The Decision to Purge

The Year the Skeletons Fell Out of the Closet

By Dana Peever

Praise

We tend to think that our life decisions are elementary. Yet many of us struggle to take action in choosing the right path forward. In her telling and deeply emotional book, Dana shares stories of everyday people who discover and confront experiences that shaped their ability to make critical life decisions. Furthermore, Dana shares a five-step system to show you how to overcome the deep-rooted psychological barriers that you may face in your everyday decisions. It's a powerful system that can apply to anyone and it's enough to change your life for the better.

~Zaid Rasid, Design Consultant

Our workplace and culture are changing at a pace never seen in recorded history. To succeed and flourish during these times of great change, which is to say, making the best decisions for you, at the right time, you need to devote time and energy to self-leadership. And you need a proven and reliable decision-making system. Through her own personal story of transformation, Dana skillfully shares her proven and powerful 5-step decision-making process. This book is a testament to the power of this process. It not only changed her own life but the lives on countless clients from all walks of life. I have come to know and love Dana for her courage, her willingness to be real and for her tremendous desire to serve others with her gifts and her story! Refreshingly real and raw, Dana shares both the drama as well as the transformation when we decide to let the skeletons out of our closet and make the decision to live our best life.

~Dieter Staudinger, Owner, Divine Transformations

This compilation of stories by Dana Peever is a true-life journey that shows how to navigate tough, painful decisions. Each story covers topics that many are afraid to explore. This book is a great companion to her 5-Step Decision Making System. Well done!

Having Dana Peever in your life is truly an authentic gift. Her keen insights and subtle perceptions are filled with empathy and compassion. No matter the issue, challenge, or decisions you are facing, Dana is well equipped to help lead you to, and support the right path for you! Her contribution to the world is priceless! I admire her strong spirit, champion her work, and, I'm honoured to call her my friend!

~Michaela Hutchison, Philanthropist/Social Entrepreneur, Community Activist

Dana's book arrived in my life in the midst of my own massive life purge requiring decision after decision. I was reminded that everyone has skeletons and aspects of their past that can unconsciously impact their current decision-making process. Her strategies are designed to help you make conscious decisions to reach the highest possibility for your life.

~Sherri Hall, Creator of Sacred Mind Method – Self Exploration Course

Dana brings a strong sense of purpose and perspective to her decision-making process. Her knowledge and style of presentation leaves you with so much confidence in her methodology. Everyone can benefit from her unique and innovative system.

~Fareen Samji, Author, Smashing the Grass Ceiling

As women of diversity, we are invited to make decisions that accommodate privilege and yet are expected to feel fortunate in having been asked at all. Dana shines the light on our strength in making confident decisions that grow our resiliency and strength. She guides us to re-learn how to make decisions for our own desires which empowers us to be healthy and thrive. These stories and Dana's approach are now part of my bundle as they are foundational in empowering all women.

~Taunya Paquette (WhiteDuck), Director, Indigenous Education, Ministry of Education, Province of Ontario

Dana and her Decision Smith System have helped guide me in making major decisions in my life and business. From moving across the country, what home to choose and what business opportunities to pursue, they have been pivotal in making solid decisions and moving forward with confidence.

~Jill Fleming, President, Tarna Technologies, Online Business Solutions

In this powerful, no-holds-barred book, Dana Peever shows what it takes to make powerful decisions that shape your destiny.

~Karen Putz, Author of Unwrapping Your Passion, Creating the Life You Truly Want

Dana is incredibly raw, honest and wise. Her app, and now book are tools that will help transform the way you make those big life decisions with confidence and strength. I was blessed to have my world collide with Dana's in my early 20's. She quickly became a mentor, friend and an inspiration to the kind of woman I wanted to become. Dana and her 5 Step System have played a role in every decision I have made the last 10 years and my life has completely shifted to one that I love to lead, emphases on the word lead!

~Amber Kelsey-Foster, General Manager of Excellence, Fitness Industry

Dana has an energy, drive and a passion for everything she does. I have had the privilege of knowing Dana for many years as a colleague, consultant, friend and trusted advisor. Her style is always challenging, interesting and with a sense of humor, intellect and wit that is truly special. Those who have the fortune to know her are better for it. Those who don't - should. Reading her work will inspire and evoke many emotions and expose the many sides of what makes Dana tick! Keep being you!

~Craig Belcher, CEO and GM

At a time in my life when I was faced with some life-changing decisions, I was fortunate enough to spend uninterrupted hours with Dana. What I appreciated most about Dana's approach was her ability to listen, and then to ask just the right questions to elicit the depth of thought required to make such decisions. Her 5 Step Decision Smith System knows no bounds. Her app is an excellent tool for anyone faced with a tough decision, starting from a very early age. This process should be taught in schools. Dana's book should be on your must-read list if you're seeking clarity at any given fork in your road. Her counsel sure helped me choose the right path!

~Nancy Fornasiero, Owner, ACE Coworking

I have known Dana on a personal and professional level for over 10 yrs. Her knowledge, work ethic, loyalty and caring nature have made her a "force" with friends and clients. Her knack of "telling it like it is" without attack or judgement is her superpower. This book will strike a chord with anyone who puts in the time to read and work through it.

~Tim Wade, Principal, Bellwoods Benefits

Dana's uncanny ability to take an in-depth look at both herself and life as a whole, offers a poignant insight into the journey that we all face. Her courageousness at asking tough questions of herself bring about a truth that is profoundly honest. Her tenacity behind her own truth is the driving force behind the person that she really is. There is something very modern about Dana. Women have fought for equality for years - juggling life, family and career. Dana makes it seem effortless, a true feminist by example. What differentiates Dana is her fearlessness, her willingness to march forward. She does not linger. She marches. I'm

vi

attracted to people who move forward, hence my complete admiration for her and everything she touches.
~Cary Mann - Owner, MillionHair Salon

A beautifully written book filled with real, raw, honest stories — Dana is the real thing. This book tells authentic stories of real people and how her Decision Making System helps anyone struggling with any decision in their life. I know first-hand her system works E.V.E.R.Y time — I truly respect her work.
~Rebecca Douros - Coaching dynamic women to connect with their soul's purpose
If anything, it may force you to examine what you're tolerating in your life.
~Steve Schulz — Entrepreneur, Author, Mentor

For years, Dana Peever has been helping people make better decisions. And not just once. She shows people a system so they can continuously make better and better choices that lead to a better life. Now she has pulled all her best strategies into the book you have in your hands. Do yourself a favor and make the decision to read this book! That will be one great decision that will lead to many many more!
~Mitch Matthews - Success Coach and creator of the DREAM THINK DO podcast

In her debut novel, Dana Peever lays it all on the line. This is a book and decision expert I highly recommend.
~Cathy Whittaker — Rotary Club President and Real Estate Agent

ISBN: 978-0-9866867-2-6
Victress Press

Contents

Their baby was delivered that weekend in a strange town, the result of the umbilical cord cutting off circulation.

All the love that mother felt for her child was strangled from her, in the tightness of the cord.

There would be no recovery.

Foreword

Decision-making is arguably one of the most important skills for us to develop in our lives. Getting stuck in indecision can paralyze a person for weeks, sometimes even years... Time spent in a half-life state with the haunting question still being asked by our minds like an irritating pop-up that never goes away, the anxiety that shows up with it, and the fearful resistance to decide which option to select, and live with.

I wonder if it's having to go through the process of taking action into the storm once we decide that we resist more, or if it's having to face regret if we get it wrong... In today's world, are we too busy to have the time to properly weigh things through? The next message or distraction mutes the question and in the absence of excruciating pain, we let time pass?

Could it be that things are more tolerable with wine?

Some choices simply suck. There is no great option to select and picking the best of the necessary evils feels like a self assigned admittance to hell. But we must do it.

Michelle Obama said, "Don't ever make decisions based on fear. Make decisions based on hope and possibility. Make decisions based on what should happen, not what shouldn't."

It fascinates me how challenging this is for so many of us to do. That even just imagining best-case versions of the future to exist in the playgrounds of our minds is something that we struggle to give permission to.

I've been studying the facets of self help, psychology, human behavior, communication, the brain, emotions and high performance for 30 years – first to figure out the out of control teenager I was and then to continuously find influence during this amazing experience we've been gifted to have as humans. I wanted to learn how to human better.

I met Dana through social media and was immediately intrigued by her decision-making system. When I work with clients to scale their businesses, increase sales or develop their leaders we inevitably end up talking about making some tough choices.

I too have a system – it's called "Performing the Exorcism" – It's Chapter 7 in my first book, *The Six Questions*. As the title implies, it's a process to decide which option to take and be done with it. It is effective and based predominantly on the feelings of each option's outcome. It's the system that I used to get through some of the toughest decisions of my life.

Learning the process of The Decision Smith (love the last name ;)) and going through it with clients to further validate their choices gave me a supercharged set of power tools that built confidence, encouraged immediate action and eliminated any essence of doubt. What a gift.

I was so impressed by this that I had Dana speak on my stage at my next leadership seminar, to teach her system to the audience herself. One of the biggest gifts we as teachers can help to equip others with is building faith in themselves. Some people resist this too, as past outcomes have proven unfortunate turns in the dots of their lives.

Everyone needs to question their faith – faith in what they believe about themselves to be true, and forgive the choices made by novice navigators who had the best of intentions, but very junior instruments. New tools or equipment make any player better – in any game... especially in life. The Decision Smith is one of these.

Hindsight, perspective, wisdom, all are earned by paying the price for their education. This is what the outcomes of our lives amount to – what we know, what we feel, what we contribute, what we've experienced, what we're connected to... the sum of our choice

And the sum of not making them. The memories in that suspended state as a younger, less equipped version of myself are so palpable. "Not making a decision is a decision". The first time I heard that statement made me catch my breath...

It's a statement I say out loud now any time I feel the resistance show up. I use Dana's system to validate my choices. Just because I'm a student and teacher of these principles does not mean I'm immune to the challenge of them. No one is.

I'm not certain that making difficult decisions ever gets *easier*... But with this tool to assist me in feeling the fear and doing it anyway, as uncomfortable as taking the tiny step might be, I have a properly vetted, mathematically calculated, scientifically constructed outcome as evidence of the rightness of the choice.

It remains to serve as proof when emotions attempt to sway me. It's become part of my "talk to the hand" routine that I give to doubt when she shows up. It's impossible to exaggerate the power that this has.

The stories in this book will unnerve you. The respect I have for their author and her quest to free those stuck in indecision is nothing short of admiration.

Michelle Obama may respect you deeply for having the courage to make choices even when they may seem impossible... but not as much as you will respect yourself.

Michell Smith,
Best Selling Author, Motivational Speaker, Sales & Leadership Expert

Introduction

I'll make this short so you can get to the good stuff. What's the last big decision you had to make? How long did it take you? Were you satisfied with the outcome? Was there a process you used to ensure you were making the right decision?

Thirty years ago, I was sitting in a psychology class at university, trying to wrap my head around the incredibly convoluted research decision matrix that had just been presented. I saw the benefits of the approach, but oh, it made my head hurt.

That lecture flipped a switch for me. When I learned that people are faced with making an average of 35,000 decisions A DAY, I just about fell off my chair. Until then, the focus had been more about navigating the consequences of my decisions, as opposed to making good ones to begin with.

So began my life's mission, to figure out a simpler approach to decision making; one that could help anyone, and to share it with the world, which is exactly what I did.

I spent years honing my own decision-making system that helped me to make exceptional decisions in my own life. Then, I applied it to interactions with clients. My 5-Step Process became a staple that I introduced to anyone struggling to make a tough decision.

The results were incredible, more far-reaching than I could have ever expected. I receive messages from people who now use my system on a regular basis, sharing the successes they have enjoyed in their lives. I've worked with students choosing post-secondary paths, seniors making real estate and financial decisions, children deciding which rep sports teams to play for, companies making hiring decisions, women deciding to leave their husbands, the list is endless.

When I launched my app, The Decision Smith, I finally introduced the world to my easy decision-making process. The five simple steps have helped people of all ages, invested in making sure they live their best life.

About five years ago, I experienced an unparalleled year as it relates to decision making. The stories that unfolded in front of me that year were exceptionally poignant, intense, and impactful, so much so it was as if the universe had a plan for me. The skeletons that fell out of the closet that year definitely needed purging.

In reflection, this book started writing itself in my mind. I vividly recall the Saturday morning I forced myself to sit down at my computer to start typing. There were chapters that had been written in my head overnight and I knew if I didn't get them down on paper my head might explode.

The result is this book: a compilation of situations faced by the women you will meet between the covers, each determined to make their best possible decision in order to move forward with confidence.

Please be prepared. There are stories of physical and sexual and emotional abuse. There are ramifications of divorce, adoption, confabulation, and unhealthy views towards money. This is a raw, deep, no-holds-barred peek into the souls of these women who finally summoned the courage to deal with their issues head-on. They finally opened the door to their skeletons. They were faced with the ultimate decision to purge; to purge the toxicity and negativity and unnecessary from their lives. Some of the outcomes are expected and some, surprising. But in the end, each woman walks away with a deeper sense of themselves, confident in the next step they've chosen to take.

All names have been changed and locations are intentionally vague. Although I have permission to share their stories, this book isn't about identifying the women. It's about identifying WITH their stories, feeling their hurt, acknowledging their pain, relating to their confusion. My greatest hope is that it will also be about rejoicing with them as you witness their journey to the other side. When I think of their stories, I picture a 'phoenix rising from ashes'.

One last thing...

When you get to the end of a book, it can be tempting to gloss over or even skip the conclusion. But please, do me a favor. Make sure you read the conclusion this time. I promise to keep it short and purposeful. It will not only reveal the silver thread woven through each of these remarkable women's stories, it will provide you with deeper insight into how YOU can make the best possible decisions in your own life. Just please, don't spoil it by reading the conclusion first.

MAKE GREAT DECISIONS AND DO LIFE FUN!

Dana

CHAPTER 1

Melissa: With Force

My conversations with Melissa will be etched in my brain forever. The stories she shared with me that *year* still make the hair on my arms stand on end. She's one strong woman and I give her so much credit for coming out the other side with such a positive outlook on life.

The summer Melissa was seven years old, her parents bought their first brand new vehicle, a silver Ford Econoline van. For two weeks, her stepfather, Paul, spent every spare minute turning the van into a mini-motorhome. He built a bed in the back for him and Melissa's mom, Rosy, complete with a cupboard at one end of the bed and a reading lamp over the other. He designed a side bed that would fold out for Sean, Melissa's younger brother, and a place on the floor for Melissa to sleep on a mattress. He even installed a padded corduroy ceiling and carpeted the inside of the van. It was the 70's, after all. This was in preparation for the drive out west that they were planning to take that July. Paul's family on his mother's side was from the west, and they were all making the trek to visit and meet many of them for the first time.

During the trip, they would drive during the day, stop along the way to do some sightseeing and visiting, and usually stay in a campground overnight. One rainy, cold

1

night when the family was about halfway to their destination, Melissa found herself with an extremely wiggly tooth. Everyone was already tucked in for the night. Her mom was reading in bed, thanks to the newly installed light. Melissa was playing with her tooth, and, when asked about the noise she was making, she showed her mom and stepfather how loose her tooth was. Rosy and Paul told her to sit up and let them pull it out. Melissa had always pulled her own teeth out when she was good and ready, and she felt extremely uncomfortable at the thought of someone else inflicting that pain on her.

But her parents were adamant. They told her it might fall out during the night and Melissa could choke. Melissa rolled her eyes while sharing the memory. To this day, she has never heard a single news report of a child choking on a tooth. No matter her protest, they insisted it be pulled out. Melissa closed her lips firmly, clenched her teeth, and refused to let them in. Her mom raised her hand, most likely intending to smack Melissa on the shoulder in exasperation. Melissa, anticipating the coming blow, simultaneously ducked her head and turned it to the side – right into her mom's striking hand. Rosy ended up smacking her daughter so hard across the face that her nose began to pour with blood. Rosy, jerking back in shock, immediately felt the bare skin of her upper back sizzle against the reading light. Melissa assumes that no one had realized how hot that little fixture would get, but it left a burn mark in the shape of a perfect circle.

Crying in pain and frustration, and not wanting to get blood in the brand-new van, Rosy opened the side door and pushed Melissa out into the rain, slamming it shut behind her. Melissa found herself alone, cold, and bloody, sitting on a soaking wet picnic table in the rain in the pitch black of the night, wearing nothing but her pajamas. I remind you she was seven years old.

After what seemed like forever, Paul emerged from the van. He took Melissa to the nearest bathroom to clean up the blood, a process that revealed the bruise beginning to form under Melissa's left eye. After she was cleaned up, Paul took Melissa back to the van and sat her in the middle seat. He grabbed a Kleenex, saying he was going to dry her tooth off so that he could get a good grip. Before she knew it, the tooth had come out without so much as a pinch. Two days later, Melissa met her great grandmother for the first time - down one tooth, and sporting a big black eye.

Spankings were a regular occurrence in their home. Melissa couldn't remember the countless times she had been shoved or thrown into her room, bottom on fire from a recent reprimand. She remembers getting out of the bathtub one night, seeing a perfectly oval bruise on her upper butt cheek. She couldn't remember running into anything or doing something to herself that would leave that kind of mark. Melissa was puzzled until she remembered the trouble she'd gotten into a few days prior when her mom had unleashed her anger on Melissa with a wooden spoon. The bruise she was now seeing was an exact replica of that spoon. Mystery solved.

Melissa and Sean were always in trouble for something. The family's dinner time had strict rules and inevitably, someone broke one of them every night. Melissa can't recall many meals at their kitchen table without someone getting into trouble, having their fingers rapped by a fork for imperfect table manners, being yelled at, or sent to their room. Dinner hour with the four of them

3

around the table was a time of fear and discomfort, one spent agonizing over what would set Paul off.

Melissa was able to pinpoint when the spankings turned exceedingly more violent. Once she became a teenager, her parents felt like they had lost some of their control over her. They resorted to increased physical violence to keep her in check, leaving Melissa petrified. Petrified to speak. Petrified to do anything for fear of upsetting her parents. Petrified of every minute she spent in their home. When she thinks back on it, Melissa wonders how she lived like that. But, she said, what choice did she have?

When Melissa was 15, she went to visit her father one weekend in early February. While there, they spent some time with one of his buddies, who asked Melissa what she wanted for Valentine's Day the following week. Melissa told him she wanted him to order her a pizza and have it sent to her at home. Valentine's Day fell on a Thursday that year - Melissa remembered it vividly. Their family was planning on going for take-out when the doorbell rang. As soon as Melissa saw the pizza delivery guy, she started laughing and recounted the story to her parents. As she brought the pizza in the house, they started taking off their coats, assuming supper had just arrived. Melissa informed them that she'd planned on saving the pizza and taking it to school the next day to enjoy with her friends at lunch. She's not sure how long the silent treatment lasted, but it was a long time.

Then there was the day just over a month later – Sunday, March 31st, a day Melissa said she will never forget. Melissa had been out with friends the night before, though she hadn't stayed out too late. Her curfew was 12:30 am, but she was tired that morning and didn't feel like doing much. Despite her wishes, Melissa was still expected to go to church. Just recently, Rosy and Paul had seemed to find God again, and they had been pushing her to spend more time at church. From Melissa's perspective, this was one area where her mom and stepfather were blind to their own sanctimony. For the previous ten years, Melissa had gone to church choir practice every week, never missing unless she was sick. Melissa was also there weekly, outside of choir, working with their minister in preparation for her upcoming confirmation. On top of that, Melissa also taught Sunday school every other week, rotating with a friend.

Since this particular Sunday happened to be her week off, she had planned to lazily take advantage of it. During the previous ten years, Paul and Rosy had come to church only when the choir was singing, which was usually on holidays and other special occasions, like Mother's Day. Recently, however, they said they had been "called back" to the church and had begun to attend more often. It didn't sit well with Melissa, after participating in church activities on a weekly basis all that time, that she was now being lectured about attending church on that particular Sunday. Melissa refused, pointing out that she'd been to church more in the last year than they had been in the last ten years combined. For Melissa, it was just another example of their hypocrisy that she could only roll her eyes at.

Her parents would not let her refusal to go to church that morning rest. They needed a reason why she wasn't going. Melissa told them it was because she'd been to church so often, she felt like it would be okay if she took a week off. That answer wasn't good enough. They asked what else was wrong, wanting to know what else was bugging her. Melissa wondered what they wanted to hear. The truth? She told them that she was tired of the way they put her sister on a pedestal. Victoria was their princess, while conversely, it felt that nothing Melissa ever did was good enough. Her parents, not surprisingly, couldn't – or wouldn't - believe that was the case. They asked her for examples, and for each one Melissa provided, they refuted with a poor excuse.

Melissa's parents asked her again what was really wrong, but she had no idea what they were fishing for. Her marks at school were fine. There were a few boys she had crushes on, but they weren't causing her any heartache. Exasperated, Melissa had told them she had no idea what they wanted her to say. They continued to push her.

At her wits' end, Melissa blurted out the first thing that came to mind. "What? Do you want me to tell you I'm pregnant?" It's worth mentioning here that Melissa shared with me that at the time, she was still a virgin. Their next words solidified how little faith they had in her. "Oh, we knew it. We knew it would always come to this. Who's the father?" Melissa looked at them, stunned, and told them she was joking. But they wouldn't let it go, they didn't believe her. That was when Melissa said things escalated into World War III. Punches were thrown. Kicks were taken.

Melissa eventually fell down the basement stairs, trying to escape their wrath, and remembers ending up at the back door. She can still clearly remember herself there, in her pajamas, a pair of plaid bottoms and a t-shirt. And she can still hear them saying "Get out," as they pushed her outside. It's important to note this occurred during the winter, in the North. Typical snow depth at that time of year was five to six feet with snowbanks towering over ten feet. Even without the wind chill, the temperature hovered around 8 degrees Fahrenheit. The roads hadn't been cleared from the overnight snowfall. Melissa knew she couldn't fight leaving, but she hoped they would take pity on her as she begged to at least put on some shoes. Her question was answered by the sound of the door locking behind her. She found herself in a situation even she couldn't have imagined: barefoot, without a coat, stranded outside in the freezing cold.

What to do? Where to go? Her best friend lived across town, too far to even consider. As her feet started to hurt in the cold snow, the closest person who came to mind was a friend who lived two blocks away. Melissa ran up the snow-filled street, sticking to the packed tire tracks, each painful barefoot step burning deeper into her soul. Melissa struggled with the reality of the incomprehensible situation she found herself in. When she finally arrived, her friend's mom answered the door. She took one look at Melissa, shook her head in surprise, ushered her inside, and quickly worked to bundle her up. She asked Melissa what had happened, to which Melissa responded that she'd gotten into a fight with her parents. She was handed a towel, and Melissa started to wipe the snow and slush from her bright red feet while her face, which was apparently covered in blood, was inspected. As her friend's mom stood over her, gently cleaning her face, Melissa brought her hand to her now-tender left shoulder. She could feel an intense, throbbing pain that coincided with the pulse of blood through her veins. By this time, Melissa's friend had joined them. Not knowing what to expect, Melissa lifted the short sleeve of her t-shirt to inspect her shoulder more carefully. They all gasped. Without question, on Melissa's shoulder lay a perfect imprint of her mother's bite, one bloody broken-skin indentation for each of her teeth. Melissa told me that, physically, the bite took a long time to heal. She's still not sure that the emotional wound ever will.

Melissa didn't want to go home and spent the next few hours at her friend's house. She eventually decided to call her grandparents, Paul's mom and dad. Melissa spent the evening with them before Paul and Rosy showed up after dinner to take her home. They didn't apologize. They didn't discuss it. They just said that it was time to come home, and that was that. It was never brought up again.

Over the next few years, Melissa spent as little time at home as possible. When she was there, it was unbearable. She felt like she was suffocating from the constant fear of doing or saying the wrong thing. She recalled another disagreement she got in with her parents. Unsure of what prompted it, she simply remembers Paul slapping her across the face. Rosy, standing there watching it all transpire, instructed him to "Get the other side to match." Paul obliged, and his second slap to Melissa's face resulted in an eventual pooling of blood at her chin. Over the next few days, the bruise turned various colors, all of which proved hard to conceal under makeup. While working her cashier shift at her part-time job, customers would sympathetically point out that she had ink on her chin. Although embarrassing, having her customers believe it was smeared ink they were seeing was far better than if they had known the truth.

Another notable incident Melissa felt important to share with me happened shortly after she graduated high school. Once again, the fallout was memorable, but what set Paul off in the first place was not - Melissa can't recall. What she does remember is it was a Saturday morning, and she had bolted to her bedroom to escape Paul's maniacal rage. Unfortunately, he caught her before she could slam the door in safety. While his anger was nothing new, Melissa felt that this time was different somehow, and sensed that even Rosy had looked afraid of what he was capable of. They had recently watched Paul push a bedroom dresser through the wall. In separate incidents, Rosy had also ducked to avoid both a hot cup of coffee and a kitchen chair that he'd launched in anger.

Melissa believes it was for that reason that Rosy somehow managed to position herself in between her husband and her daughter, precariously lodged in the bedroom doorway. Paul still had a grip on Melissa's left arm, and he had begun twisting. And twisting. And twisting. Just as Melissa thought her arm couldn't withstand another second, Rosy finally lost her footing and the trio tumbled into Melissa's room. Melissa scrambled up onto her bed, trying to escape Paul as he lunged after her. In an instant, he had flipped her over and was hovering above her, squeezing her arms as he held her tightly against the bed.

Melissa can still remember the sound of him screaming obscenities at her, can still feel the spittle flying from his mouth landing sickeningly on her face, can still smell his hot, vile breath. She was truly afraid for her life and did the only thing she could think to do at the time. Melissa bent her knee back as far as it would go, bringing it close to her chin, then propelled her leg forward with all the force she could muster. It was a bullseye. Her right foot landed squarely between his legs. As the pain registered in his eyes, Paul finally rolled off of her, writhing in agony.

Melissa still had to work that day. She arrived for her shift with cuts on her face, an injured arm, and more bruises than she could count. If she'd been considering it before, the incident that morning had removed all doubt from Melissa's mind. She'd finally made the decision to leave home and was beginning to mentally work through her different options.

Before she left for work, Rosy told her to come home right after her shift so they could discuss what had happened. Obligingly, Melissa was home by four, but her mom and Paul didn't sit down to speak with her until seven o'clock that evening. When they did, it wasn't a discussion they were interested in having. Instead, they presented Melissa with the laundry list of rules she would have to abide by if she wanted to continue living under their roof. Among their conditions: Melissa had to get a 'real' job, which meant it had to come with a strict nine to five schedule; she had to find somewhere to volunteer regularly; she could only see her boyfriend once a week, and was limited to once weekly phone calls with him, as well. The list went on, and on, and on. As she listened to them drone on, Melissa found herself nodding along with the ridiculous stipulations, each one an additional attempt at regaining the control they'd lost. She hoped her parents thought she was nodding in agreement, but inside, their list only reaffirmed her decision to leave. Melissa knew her days there were numbered, and that she would be moving out as soon as she could.

On top of the day she'd had, Melissa and her boyfriend had plans with his family that evening. Melissa reminded Rosy and Paul that she would be staying overnight at his home, something she had done many times before. But this time, Paul disagreed and told her, "If

10

you don't come home tonight, don't ever come home again." Rosy interjected, pleading with Paul to stop speaking. "Don't say that. You know what will happen." Melissa, having made her decision, replied, "Fine."

She left for her boyfriend's and spent the night there. While her family was at church the next day, she packed her things and stayed with her boyfriend again that night. On Monday, she was a girl on a mission. By the end of the day, Melissa had found a full-time job and an apartment, and from there, she never looked back.

That same Monday, Melissa also called the therapist that her family had started seeing together a few months earlier. By that point, things had been bad enough for the family that outside intervention was required, but in Melissa's opinion, it wasn't doing much good. The counselor would talk to Paul and Rosy, either alone or with the kids in the room. The kids were terrified to say anything to the therapist in front of their parents, as they knew there would be hell to pay at home if they did. They just nodded and agreed with whatever was said.

Melissa was able to get an appointment with the therapist the next day. When she showed up at his office that afternoon, his shock upon seeing her was visible. He asked Melissa what had happened, appraising her injuries - those he could see - as he spoke. Melissa explained that she'd gotten into a fight with Paul a few days prior, briefly describing the altercation, their subsequent rules and her resulting exit, telling him she hadn't gone back home since. Melissa's therapist explained that she needed to see her family doctor as soon as possible, for two reasons: to ensure she was okay and to ensure there was a record of her injuries. Melissa was uncomfortable with the suggestion, even though she knew that the therapist was right. "I don't want to see a doctor, because he would have to report it," she had explained in a small voice. The therapist assured her that, because Melissa was over eighteen, the doctor would not have the duty to report.

Taking the therapist's advice, based on his assurances, Melissa scheduled the next available appointment with her family doctor. Much like the therapist, he took one look at her and wanted to know exactly what had happened. As Melissa explained, her doctor made notes of all her cuts and bruises, spending extra time documenting those on her face. After inspecting her injured arm, the doctor determined that Paul had torn ligaments when he'd ruthlessly twisted it in her bedroom doorway. Throughout the appointment, even as he spoke to Melissa, her doctor continued taking notes. As her appointment wrapped up, he dropped a bomb on her. Because there were younger siblings in the home under the age of sixteen, he had to report it.

Melissa didn't need to see into the future to know how everything was going to go down.

Children's Aid was called, as was required by her doctor. She learned that they completed a home visit with a mortified Paul and Rosy. Their only question for Melissa centered around understanding why she'd contacted Children's Aid. Melissa explained how things had transpired, that she hadn't been the one who placed the call, but they never believed her. Her parents told her to stay off their property and forbade her having any contact with her younger siblings. It was two years before Melissa would speak to them again.

Fast forward fifteen years, tensions remained high in Melissa's relationship with her parents. They were, at least, on speaking terms. Melissa had since finished university, gotten married and she and her husband, Jeff, had welcomed two wonderful children.

By that time in his life, Paul had become fully engrossed in golf. Everything was golf in Paul's world, and everyone who knew him knew it. For as long as Melissa had known him, Paul had been that way. As soon as he became interested in something, that was it, he was all in. Any hobby that caught his fancy became all-consuming, like an obsession, or a fixation. This was such a well-known trait of Paul's that it had become an inside joke for the family, to wonder what his next fascination would be. When her kids were young, Melissa lost count of the times Rosy showed up for a visit sans Paul, only to explain that he couldn't make it because he was golfing. Melissa can't say that she was sorry about his absence. He missed some great times with her kids, but that wasn't her issue.

When Melissa's son, Brooks, turned five, he received a new set of golf clubs from Paul and Rosy. The golf course Paul kept a membership at offered Junior Lessons during the summer, and as part of his birthday gift, they invited Brooks to spend a week with them that summer and take lessons.

Before deciding if Brooks could go, Melissa and her husband, Jeff, discussed the visit at length. It would be their son's first extended time with Paul and Rosy, and he would be on his own with them. Melissa was, understandably, worried. She feared they would get mad at him, and in their anger, resort to the same kind of physical punishment that she'd known as a child. Their brand of discipline was the polar opposite of how she and Jeff chose to resolve conflict in their home. Melissa didn't know how Brooks would react if he was put in a situation like that, and she didn't know what to expect from her parents. Trust was hard, even after so much time had passed. She and Jeff decided to let Brooks go, making him promise to call home immediately if he ever felt the least bit uncomfortable. In the end, Melissa says, she found a way to trust them. To trust that they had changed - enough, at least, to keep the past's bad behavior where it belonged.

Brooks was easygoing, the kind of kid who let most things roll off of his back. At the end of the week, he came home saying he'd had a good time. After speaking to her son, Melissa felt confident that nothing had happened that she needed to be worried about. Brooks seemed genuinely excited about all the fun things he did while he was visiting his grandparents.

The following year, when Brooks was again invited to visit his grandparents over the summer, the decision to let him go was much easier to make. She and Jeff made arrangements for his trip, and off he went. When Melissa met Rosy to pick Brooks up at the end of the week, she was expecting another positive report. Instead, Rosy informed Melissa that her six-year-old son's behavior at Golf Camp hadn't been as good as expected and that he had embarrassed Papa Paul. Melissa wasn't thrilled with the report, and resisted the urge to engage with her mother, wondering what kind of behavior she and Paul had expected from their six-year-old grandson. Melissa waited until she could speak privately with her son. When she asked him what the week had been like, Brooks told her that camp was boring a few times and confessed that he hadn't listened as well as he could have. While Melissa is not one to excuse away her children's bad behavior, she didn't see much of an issue with Brooks' behavior at Golf

Camp. He was six! And, if Paul was worried about his reputation, that was his issue to deal with.

When Brooks turned seven, he received a birthday card from his grandparents in the mail. Once again, he was invited to come to Golf Camp that summer as part of his gift. Unlike the prior two years, however, this invitation came with a stipulation. "If you think you can behave yourself for the entire week," the seven-year-old's birthday card read. Melissa immediately called Rosy to inform her that Brooks would not be joining them for Golf Camp that year. How could she ask her son to spend a week with his grandparents, knowing he would be worried about his behavior and about disappointing them, the entire time? Melissa knew how inadequate it had felt, to see herself through their eyes and she would never put Brooks in a position where he would risk feeling the same way. Jeff would take Brooks out golfing, and they'd find a local golf camp for him to attend that summer.

A few weeks later, Rosy called to inform Melissa that it had hurt her deeply that Jeff was going to take Brooks out golfing. Melissa explained - to her own mother - that it was her job, as Brooks' mother, to look out for him, and his best interests. And that was what she was doing.

On Brooks' eighth birthday, another card came in the mail, and with it, another invitation to Golf Camp. Jeff and Melissa decided to get their son's perspective. When they had asked Brooks if he would like to go that summer, he told them he would and felt he would be able to behave himself while he was there. Melissa met Rosy half-way to drop Brooks off. As she was saying good-bye to her son, Melissa told him to please be good. With a straight face, Rosy looked at her and said, "If he's not, I'll just beat him."

15

Melissa was shocked. It was all she could do not to grab Brooks and pull him away from his grandmother, and from her insanity. She couldn't believe Rosy could joke about something like that. Melissa looked at Brooks and he nodded. They'd had many discussions about him visiting his grandparents, and about what kind of behavior was and was not appropriate from Rosy and Paul. He knew what deserved a phone call home. That nod was her son letting her know she didn't have to worry about him. He would behave. And call if he needed.

It was an anxious week for Melissa and Jeff waiting for Brooks to come home. While he was away, they engaged in more lengthy discussions about how to move forward with their children and Melissa's parents. Brooks returned from his visit with reports of good behavior and had nothing unusual to share after coming home. But, Melissa could not get Rosy's comment out of her head. Melissa knew she needed to discuss it with Rosy before she could put it behind her.

At first, Rosy said she didn't know what Melissa was talking about. Then, she tried to pass her comment off as a harmless joke. But Melissa wasn't ready to accept her mother's deflection or excuse so easily. She told her mother that considering the way she had been raised, her comment was unacceptable. Again, Rosy pretended she didn't know what Melissa was referring to, forcing her to remind her mother of the physical abuse she'd endured growing up. Instead of apologizing, Rosy told her daughter that she was crazy, and went on to share a story to prove what she felt was a valid point.

Rosy told her daughter she had recently looked after her neighbor's infant. As the parents were leaving, they had said, 'I hope she's good for you.' And Rosy had replied 'Well, if she's not, I'll just beat her.'

Melissa was mortified and shocked at her mother's ignorance. She told Rosy she couldn't say those things. But Rosy could not, or would not, relate to where her daughter was coming from. The next time they were on the phone, Rosy told Melissa she'd been thinking about their last conversation. For a moment, Melissa thought maybe her mother had an epiphany. Then Rosy spoke. "You know, the way you approached that subject really put me on the defensive. You have to learn to talk to people more delicately. You'll get a lot more out of your conversations."

Since then, further requests for visits with the grandparents have been extended which prompted Melissa's desire to discuss her options with me. Melissa did not feel a sense of closure with her mother on the topic, and this had continued to keep her up at night.

On one hand, we discussed the fact that she didn't want to impede her children's' ability to build a relationship with their grandparents. Alternatively, she would never forgive herself if her kids ever received any physical punishment at the hands of her parents.

As we waded through the various scenarios and factors she was considering, it became clear to Melissa that her first priority was to her kids. Visits have since become fewer and farther between. And when they do visit their grandparents, Melissa and Jeff prepare them in advance. They arrive equipped with an arsenal of what to expect and how to counter each blow, should the need arise.

CHAPTER 2

Tracy (Part 1): Just Getting Started

Tracy was a client I met with many times that *year*. It took a few weeks for her to share her history before we could dig into how she would move forward. This is her story.

Her parents divorced when she was young and she went on to live with her mom, Wendy, her stepfather, Chuck, and their kids, Nick and Lori.

Wendy and Chuck were extremely strict, and Tracy revealed that things declined exponentially the older she grew. She had recently come to realize how bad things were at an early age, something she had not recognized as a child.

One weekend, Tracy and her brother, Nick, decided to surprise Chuck and Wendy with breakfast in bed. They were so proud of the masterpiece they'd lovingly prepared. She didn't remember everything they made, but she was certain there was toast. And the reason she knew there was toast was because she'll never forget the sound of Chuck's accusatory voice as he grumbled, "When you make toast, you need to butter it all the way to the edge. Otherwise, it's hard and crusty like this piece that I can't eat."

When Tracy was eleven, a friend of Wendy's had surgery and needed some assistance looking after her kids. Wendy offered to take in the daughter, Candice, a girl who was Tracy's age and went to her school, but not someone who she had ever had a conversation with outside of the visits their mothers shared.

The expectation was that Tracy would willingly and happily allow a second bed for Candice to be squeezed into her already small room. And, what came next still baffles her. Tracy was forced to open her closet to Candice and allow her to wear any of her clothes that she wanted. She guessed her parents felt that Candice was not as fortunate. The questions Tracy got from her friends about why someone else was wearing her clothes still echo in her mind.

Three other things occurred during this time that forced Tracy to realize that Wendy did not have her back, as a young girl might expect her mom to.

As Candice was getting ready to go on her annual school trip Wendy didn't believe Candice had enough clothes to take so she bought her more.

Each year, they had a big project due in school. And each year, Wendy had helped Tracy tremendously in preparing for her project. But that year was different. Wendy spent all her time helping Candice with her project and said she'd helped Tracy enough over the years, it was time she did it on her own. Tracy should have been used to such tough love, but she was unprepared for the complete dismissal.

The third memory she shared of Candice was a time they had practiced back bridges in the living room. They were entertaining company, and Wendy was smiling proudly, commenting on how Candice was doing bridges perfectly, while Tracy struggled. She searched for reassurance from her mother and asked her mom how she thought she was doing. Wendy laughed and told her she would never be as flexible as Candice. It was the first time she remembered her mother voicing that someone was better than her own child. Tracy didn't know why it affected her so greatly. She guessed she had believed that your mom should be the one person in the world who would always choose you, or at least let you down gently. That you would always get her vote. That moment left her feeling exceptionally lonely.

In recounting these stories to me as an adult, Tracy acknowledged that they seemed trivial, but the hurt she had experienced at the time and carried with her into early adulthood was very real.

Every girl in her early tweens experiences changes in her hormones, the advent of a monthly visit Tracy described as a mostly unwelcome friend. Tracy remembered it like it was yesterday. And while most kids she knew ran to their mothers for assistance and support, she simply went to the cupboard where she'd stored the "starter pack" she had ordered for free. It wasn't until she was running out of supplies that she had to tell Wendy. It was then that she told her mom it wasn't the first time dismissing any further conversation or input about it.

Tracy's relationship with her mother was already in a sad state. If there was one time in a young girl's life when she should feel comfortable going to her mother, that should be it. Already at twelve years of age, Wendy was the last person Tracy wanted to talk to.

It was around that time when she began to recognize why she didn't like being at home. She understands now that much of Chuck and Wendy's actions stemmed from their own dysfunctions. She told me she doesn't blame them and shared that she intentionally chose not to emulate or accept that behavior in her own life.

Tracy went on to share that during her early teens, her stepfather, Chuck, had taken up the sport of Ultralight Flying - essentially a hang glider with a small engine. After supper each night, he would pack up his stuff and head out to the shop. A farmer had rented him a hangar and run-way about ten minutes from their house. The main floor of the hangar was a workshop where Chuck stored his ultralights. He converted the upstairs to a classroom where he taught others how to fly as well.

Tracy felt inclined to join him to escape the oppression of the house. And so, it became their routine almost every night. It was the most connection they ever had. But, even after all the time she spent with him there, everyone else in the family got a ride in his ultralight. But not her. By the time he was comfortable enough to take passengers up, they were on the outs.

She thinks it was around the same time Chuck and Wendy told her they bought a motorcycle as a second vehicle for Chuck to get to work. Tracy had told them it was the most ridiculous thing she had ever heard. A family of five with a motorcycle as a second vehicle in a town where the snow started in October and many times wasn't gone until May. Everyone got a ride on it but her. And after they sold it a few short years later, she overheard them say it was the dumbest purchase they had ever made.

As she continued to share her history with me, Tracy vividly recalled a summer when her Uncle Eric and Aunt Laura, Wendy's younger sister, had arrived for a visit.

While they were at Tracy's house, Laura was helping to clean up and put some cheese away in the fridge. After they left, Wendy was searching for the cheese, not able to find it in its normal spot. Tracy remembers it specifically being a package of Kraft Cheese Slices with more than half the package used. Her aunt had folded the empty side of the package underneath the still full side, leaving it a square shape. When Wendy finally found the cheese, she was livid at how disrespectful her sister had been in not putting the cheese away in the right spot.

Tracy recalls how perplexed she felt about her mom's anger, evidenced by her subsequent actions when they traveled to her grandparents' cottage a few days later. Aunt Laura and Uncle Eric had already arrived in their van with their four kids and a neighbor of theirs, Shawna, a girl just a bit older than Tracy, whom she'd met a few times before. They spent a lot of time together that week. Tracy was the oldest grandchild by a few years, so it was nice to have another teenager to hang around with. They talked, and listened to Loverboy on repeat. And, it was during their talks that Tracy shared with Shawna how upset Wendy had become over her sister not putting the cheese away in the right spot. They were both stymied by her over-the-top reaction.

As a teenager, you pour your heart out to your friends and you believe it forms an unbreakable bond that will last your lifetime. Her time with Shawna was like that, but what she hadn't considered was that her new friend had known her aunt much longer, ergo a greater allegiance to her. Tracy does not fault her for it. It's a lesson that takes most people years to learn. And so, the story Tracy told her new 'best' friend about the cheese made its way to her aunt, and then to Wendy which is when the proverbial shit hit the fan.

Tracy told me she didn't remember how long she was grounded that time. She was told that whatever happens in their house stays in their house and that she was never to mention to anyone, ever, what went on between their four walls. That was their private family time, and no one needed to know anything their family said behind closed doors. In recounting this story to me, I watched Tracy shake her head in amazement, all these years later.

Tracy had begun to observe ongoing hypocrisy in her family. They were expected to portray a perfect family life to the public. And, by that time, Chuck and Wendy's relationship was well past the honeymoon stage. They were married the summer after Tracy's younger sister, Lori, was born. And it wasn't long before she could see the signs of a relationship in trouble. The yelling was incessant, and Tracy went on to say that her childhood seemed to be one screaming match after another. Tracy vowed she would work towards more peace and harmony in her own home; not because she felt she had to be better than them. She could not imagine living her life that way, by choice.

She tries to keep in mind good memories too, like the time Wendy spent making skating costumes for the Annual Skating Carnival, all the time she spent sewing and knitting for them as kids. She talked about how Chuck made candy apples every year for Halloween, a tradition she has since carried on. But she does not remember much else and told me she wonders if she may have blocked the good to focus on the bad for some deep-rooted reason.

Tracy was actively involved in her church. She was on Student Council at school, played volleyball, ran cross-country and was in the school play one year. She became involved in Studio 132, a group of students who put together little comedy sketches for their monthly assemblies, à la Saturday Night Live. She babysat and spent time with friends.

Tracy's town was where the main high school was and considered the mecca where most weekend activities took place. And the friends she hung around with most, lived in outlying towns. Wendy and Chuck let her have friends sleep over quite often. It was a win for both her and her friends. They got to stay in town and go to the same parties. And, Tracy's friends acted as buffers minimizing her interaction with the rest of the family. She declared that she was a girl with a purpose even back then.

She dated a few boys, spent time with friends, always had a part-time job, and went home only to sleep. Tracy described herself as a good kid overall, but she stretched some boundaries. When she did go out, she had very strict curfews. If she was just one minute late, she was grounded the next weekend.

Tracy and her bestie, Rachel, used to help themselves to Chuck's beer stash most weekends. They'd drink under the bridge and then buy watermelon bubblegum at the convenience store. One night, Chuck happened to walk into the store while they were there. Tracy ducked outside to wait for Rachel and they quickly stuffed their mouths with gum so Chuck wouldn't be able to smell beer on their breath. He questioned the overwhelming smell of watermelon and asked what they were trying to hide. He didn't seem satisfied with their answer, but he left and off they went to their party.

There was a weekend one winter when a friend, from where her dad lived three hours away, was finally allowed to visit. And anyone who knew anything about visitors to their town at their age knew your time was not complete without a visit across the border where the drinking age was a year younger. Tracy was dating a guy at the time who had a car and he brought a friend along. The four of them drove across the border and had a rocking time dancing the night away. But someone had to be the responsible one so Tracy appointed herself the designated driver and did not drink any alcohol that night.

Living with Wendy and Chuck meant that Tracy and her friend had a curfew. And as they were driving home, Tracy realized they were going to be late. They decided to stop to call Chuck and tell him that they'd been watching movies at the friend's and when they came out, her boyfriend's car wouldn't start. That way they might be able to get around being late for curfew. Chuck drove out to get them. When he arrived, he was full of suspicion. He wondered where the car was that wouldn't start and questioned the fact that Tracy and her friend both got in the back seat, making him feel like a taxi driver.

Upon arrival at home, he and Wendy decided to question them separately. But Tracy knew they would probably find out the truth anyway, so she outright admitted they'd gone to the bar, that she had driven her boyfriend's car, and they started home without enough time to spare. That's why they were late.

And then they questioned her friend. At that point, Tracy told me about her friend's alcohol consumption that night compared to hers. Actually, there was no comparison. Tracy had nothing, her friend had lots. Tracy recounted it all lightheartedly as she had been truly thrilled at how the evening unfolded until she realized they'd be late. Her goal had been to show her girlfriend a great time and she had succeeded. Tracy likes to think that what happened next was because of her friend's inebriation. She told Chuck and Wendy that Tracy had been drinking the entire night and that she hadn't had a drop. They believed her friend.

As punishment, her parents decided she could not go to an annual curling bonspiel that she attended each year - the mother of all punishments. She told me they could not have taken away anything worse, and they knew it. So, Tracy learned that telling the truth to them had no benefit.

In her junior year of high school, Tracy started dating a wonderful guy. The relationship made her feel special. They spent weekends at his cottage. His parents and brother always treated her well. It was heaven to spend time with him and his family and she did it as often as she could. His dad would make him wash the car before he took her on dates. He took her to Prom. They drove back roads in his old pick-up truck. They fell in love. And then, she said, the bottom fell out of her life.

Chuck and Wendy shared the news that Chuck had received a promotion at work, which was great for him but required a move to a town four and a half hours away. It was already decided. The plan was to move that July. Tracy was devastated. She was moving away from a town she'd lived in for eleven years. She was to simply pick up and start a new school in senior year.

She remembered feeling as though she wouldn't survive it. She didn't want new friends - she liked the ones she had. And, she had a boyfriend - what would happen to that? Tracy struggled with the idea of the move but because she had a summer job, it was decided she could stay an extra month with her grandparents and move just before school started.

When her parents came to pick her up at the end of the summer, Tracy was not prepared to leave her town, her friends, her boyfriend, her comfort zone. They expected her to move to a new town where the only people she knew were the four people who she actively tried to spend the least amount of time with.

We decided to wrap things up for this session. I could feel the hurt Tracy was being forced to relive as the pain of these stories resurfaced. I was hoping she'd go home and find her Calgon, whether that was in a bathtub or a wine glass.

CHAPTER 3

Ann: The Root of All Evil

A nn visited my office that *year* for the first time. During the first five minutes of our conversation, she acknowledged that money had always held negative connotations in her life. She knew she was doing alright for herself financially, but she still harbored some apprehension.

Her earliest memories about money highlighted her mother as a key figure. Payday was on Thursdays when her father would cash his check at the bank after work. Ann remembered how, upon arriving home every Thursday, he would hand her mother cash for the week's bills. A long time ago, it seemed to her, in retrospect.

On these nights, after supper, Ann and her mother made their weekly trip to the grocery store. In the early days, Ann remembers a strict $25 budget for the week's groceries – to feed a family of five! In those days, Ann would be given the task of finding something specific on the list. Each time, upon arriving back with the item and before placing it in the cart, it became routine for her to tell her mother exactly how much it cost, to the penny. Her mother would keep a running tally, and in the event they ever went over budget, they'd have to put things back. There was literally no room to spare.

From a young age, Ann earned an allowance for completing various weekly household chores. As early as six years old, she clearly remembers having to use a stool to reach the sink to do the dishes. Ultimately, she was responsible for doing the supper dishes every night and sweeping the kitchen floor afterward. She made her own bed, her parents' bed, and her sister's bed every morning, changing the sheets once a week before school. Ann dusted and vacuumed weekly until her younger brother was old enough to help, and cleaned the bathroom. She washed the floors once a month. Not only did she have her plate full with chores, but she had to complete them on a strict deadline – one that had as much wiggle room as their grocery budget. All chores had to be done by the time her parents got home each Friday at 5 pm. If they weren't finished, there were huge consequences, which Ann learned from experience on more than one occasion. If dishes weren't done to their satisfaction – and their satisfaction was often subject to inspection – she might find herself unloading the dishwasher to wash each dish by hand. Likewise, if her dusting wasn't perfect, Ann would find herself dusting the whole house again.

As Ann got older and her schedule became more complicated, she learned the hard way that it was each man for himself in her household. There was one day each week when extracurricular activities kept her particularly busy. She wouldn't arrive home from school until after 7:30 pm, having left at 8:30 am those mornings. Even on these nights when she'd eaten elsewhere, upon arriving home, Ann could count on being greeted by her family's dirty dishes, and by her family – who were generally seated around the television set. I could see in Ann's eyes how much those memories bothered her, even to this day.

I asked Ann what her weekly allowance was, in exchange for her hard work. She smiled as she admitted it had started out at $2 a week and remained there for many years. Why the smile? One night, Ann's father had a friend over for a few drinks and to play cards. He asked how much allowance Ann received and it was that night that she received her first-ever raise. Ann doubled her earnings and started making $4 a week.

Adding to Ann's burden of responsibility at home, she began babysitting her younger siblings when she was eleven. This became another component of her household chores and was not something she was paid for. In high school, Ann was allowed one "free" night each weekend to go out and was expected to babysit the other night. If their plans overlapped and fell on the same night, it was Ann who was responsible for securing and paying a babysitter for her younger siblings.

During the summer months, Ann earned a little extra money by packing her father's lunch, a service for which he paid her 25 cents a day. Invariably, he would ask if she wanted to play cards on the weekend for money and he would win it all back. Somehow, she never learned.

Ann couldn't recall a single instance of her family talking about money in a good or positive way. Clothing purchases were often made on her mother's lunch hour at The "GT" Boutique, a cheap chain of small department stores selling knock-offs, just the thing a teenager wanted to show up to school wearing. Their family's conversations always centered on scarcity – the theme seemed to be that they never had enough. Once Ann was old enough to work and make her own money, life became her responsibility. She received the necessities from her parents, but not much else. As she grew older, her parents were promoted in their jobs, so money became less of a burden, but the roots of evil had already been planted.

As Ann was nearing university age, she specifically recalled a conversation she'd had with her mother in passing one morning. "Hey Ann," she had said casually. "Dad and I had a decision to make - to send you to university or put in a pool. They are coming to dig the pool next week."

Ann wasn't sure if her mother was trying to be funny in sharing the news this way, but it made her realize how financially alone she was going to be from that point on. At the time, she wasn't aware of how prophetic her thoughts would be. Before she even started university, she would be living on her own, and not by choice. Things became unbearable with all of them under the same roof. Ultimately, Ann was left to find new living arrangements in short order.

She described for me the two full-time jobs she worked leading up to starting school that fall. One was during the day as a pharmaceutical technician and the other, by night, as a nanny for a young boy and infant girl whose mother had been in a car accident. After covering regular living expenses for six months, she knew she wouldn't have enough saved for the entire school year. That left her with no recourse but to apply for financial assistance. Her parents, in characteristic fashion, refused to sign any of the forms required for her to be able to apply through normal channels. Because of this, Ann had to file a serious family rift in order to apply for assistance, indicating that her parents were refusing to assist with school costs. After she filed her paperwork, the financial assistance office reached out to Ann's parents for their reasoning. In response, they indicated that they weren't

32

willing to co-sign a loan or fill out any documentation on Ann's behalf, but they conceded to writing a letter explaining their stance, indicating they didn't want to impede Ann's ability to get an education. That sounded contradictory in Ann's opinion, as they knew she required the forms to receive any assistance.

She divulged to me that she still isn't sure that her parents ever knew that she received a copy of the letter they wrote from her financial aid administrator. What she is sure of is her memory of that moment, how hollowly and achingly alone reading the letter had made her feel. It gave her insight into the depth of her parents' vindictiveness and malevolence, and it wasn't appealing.

Ann did receive financial assistance, but it wasn't a lot. There were weeks when she survived on a single box of macaroni and cheese, stretched out to last. There really were some tough times. Once she got settled, she was able to take on a part-time job which certainly assisted with bills.

When Ann left home, her parents had removed her from all medical benefit plans immediately and made sure that she was fully aware. At the time, it had felt like another turn of the blade in her back. To be safe, Ann had purchased her own coverage while in university, at an exorbitant cost, especially for a student. In the spring of her second year, Ann learned that she needed to have her wisdom teeth removed. Her drug plan would cover the cost in full, but there was a catch – Ann would need to pay for the procedure upfront, and then be reimbursed by her insurance provider.

Like most students, Ann didn't have $1000 simply lying around, so she summoned up the courage to call her parents to ask if they would consider lending her the cash.

She promised that, as soon as she was reimbursed, she would sign the check right over to them. In a manner that still puzzles Ann, they reluctantly agreed to lend her the money for the procedure. As expected, there were invisible and unpredictable strings attached. Not long after Ann's teeth had been removed, while she was still waiting for the reimbursement check, Ann mentioned to her mother that she'd been out for dinner with friends the night before. Ann's mother's demeanor immediately shifted to one of irritation. Quickly and not-so-subtly, she reminded Ann that she owed them money, and shouldn't be going out for dinner until they'd been reimbursed. Money was always a battle with them.

As Ann was nearing graduation, she promised herself a special reward. To commemorate all the hard work and effort she'd put into getting her degree on her own, Ann had proudly decided to purchase herself a school ring. Nearing the end of her final year, Ann's mother called to let her know they had decided to buy her a school ring as a graduation gift. Ann had simply replied, "No thanks. It is going to be a gift to myself." When graduation finally arrived, they presented Ann with a generous gift for which she was extremely thankful, a check for $5000. Her parents told her they thought Ann could put the money towards the sizeable debt she'd accumulated from her years of student loans.

Not surprisingly, this didn't sit well with Ann. Throughout university, she'd endured a ton of financial hardship, much of it due to her parents' refusal to offer any assistance whatsoever. It wasn't because they weren't able. While she was at university, they'd completed a $40,000 house renovation (close to $70,000 in today's numbers), plus taken countless trips over the years, so they had plenty of money. It was where they chose to spend it that defeated Ann. Here she was, proud beneficiary of $45,000 in student loan debt (almost $80,000 today), with many thousands already forgiven through the bursaries and scholarships she'd earned. She knew it would be a long time before she paid it all off, but putting herself through university was something that she'd decided she was going to take full credit for. No one else could have that honor.

Ultimately, Ann decided to use the gift of money from her parents to help with a down payment on her first house. Ann's mother wasn't happy when she learned of her daughter's decision and said the money had been intended for school. Ann's angered reply was equally pointed. "If the condition of accepting the money was that it had to go to student loans, then the check should have been made out to the bank."

Ann also informed her mother that, in considering interest rates for student loans versus interest rates for mortgages, it made much more sense to use it for a down payment. Ann knew that her mother understood the math, but it never sat well with her. The bottom line was simple: Ann would never give her parents the opportunity to say they helped pay for her education. She'd had to scratch and claw for every penny. Deep down, Ann felt this was their subconscious way of making themselves feel less guilty about what they'd done. She wasn't letting them off the hook this time.

Subsequently, when both her brother and sister attended post-secondary school, Ann said she'd give me one guess as to who foot the bill. Unbeknownst to her at the time, I'm sure that took a toll on Ann's self-confidence and self-worth, as well as her importance in the hierarchy of her family.

While still in school, Ann learned that their former family dentist was selling his well-loved but in great condition, Honda, for $2400. Having had to rely on public transport, friends, and family for rides until then, Ann thought this would be a good investment. She test drove it and knew, because of their familiarity, that he wouldn't sell her a lemon. The issue was not the car – it was finding the money to buy it. Rather than miss the opportunity, Ann swallowed her pride and called her parents to ask for a loan, which she would repay with interest. The answer was a definitive no. No explanation offered beyond that – just, NO.

Years later, Ann's younger sister declared bankruptcy because an ex-boyfriend had left her high and dry with more bills than she could pay. At that time, a person declaring bankruptcy could own a car with up to a $5000 value. Ann heard through the grapevine that her parents bought her sister a car worth exactly $5000, so she would have some form of transportation. When her sister was feeling homesick, her parents didn't think twice about buying her a plane ticket home. When Ann's younger brother got married, they bought them a digital camera as a present. When they learned that he didn't have a computer to download the pictures to, they bought them one as well. Ann wouldn't have minded a new computer or a flight somewhere. She presented these anecdotes to her mother during a heated discussion about why she felt like an outsider in own her family, and how she was always treated differently. Her mother's response? That they were keeping a tally and everything would all come out evenly in their will.

The last time Ann ever addressed the topic of money with her parents was when she and her husband had started building a new home for their family. In talking with their mortgage broker, they realized there was a chance of them being a bit short on closing funds. One last time, Ann swallowed her pride and asked her parents if they would consider giving her a loan, should it become necessary. By now, you can probably guess the answer. Undefeated, they went to her husband's parents, who immediately offered to be on standby, no strings attached. After moving into their new home, Ann's mother nosily asked what had happened with the money. Ann simply told her that their mortgage broker had miscalculated and that they had been fine. It didn't surprise me to hear that a few years later, when Ann's younger sister was in the market for a house but didn't have the funds or the credit rating, that Ann's parents co-signed for her.

Recounting two quick stories before making any final decisions about how to move forward, Ann identified they had taken place when she was in her early 40's. They drove home her point of the lasting and negative effects her parents' beliefs about money had on her entire life to that point. Ann and her husband had been working on their backyard and had purchased a brand-new hot tub. Her dad had called and she was excited to tell him about their upcoming delivery. His response was completely unexpected. "How much did it cost?" he had asked as if it was any of his business. It was his first question. Not what brand, how big, when's it coming? She described how relentless he was with his questioning until she told him to the exact penny how much they'd paid. I watched Ann subtly shake her head as she finished that story.

Finally, with excitement, she described for me the day she paid cash for her dream vehicle. It was one she'd had her eyes set on for years. When she'd test driven one a few years prior, the sales guy at the dealership had given her the impression he never thought she'd be able to afford one. Well, here she was, pleased as punch with herself and her purchase. Within the week, they found themselves driving it to pick up the kids from their grandparents where they'd been visiting. When Ann's mother saw the vehicle, the first question she asked was, "How much did THAT cost?" Sound familiar? Not a congratulations, wow, that's great, holy smokes, nothing. How much did it cost? Ann's short response: "A lot." Undeterred, when Ann was out of earshot, her mother approached her husband to see if he would divulge how much she'd paid for the vehicle. The whole memory still made Ann squint in disbelief of it having transpired.

Ann knew that her parents' muddled ideas about money, if left unchecked, could continue to propagate a potentially unhealthy approach to her own finances. She'd been conscious of it over the years, but as her kids grew, she wondered if her misguided ideas would permeate their consciousness. She could cross her fingers and hope that this simple acknowledgment would prevent her damaged views from trickling down to her kids. Or, what I reinforced was probably a much more plausible option, she could choose to move forward in a very intentional manner as it related to money. Factoring in the incredible opportunity she had to set a different stage for her kids, she made the decision that day to approach anything money-related with an abundance mindset. She would be cognizant of the language she used in front of them, never addressing it with scarcity, reminding them of the value when spending, but framing the topic in a much more positive light than she grew up with. She would emancipate herself from the burden of her parents' dysfunction, once and for all.

CHAPTER 4

Rebecca (Part 1): Way Too Young

I would be remiss not to share the fact that Rebecca's story goes back years. The more conversations we had, the more I discovered how deeply her parents' divorce had impacted her. That *year* seemed to have taken more of a toll on her than usual and she finally decided to seek clarity. I condensed her story into two chapters, hoping that I captured all the nuances sufficiently.

Rebecca's mom, Charlene, and her father, Ryan, met in high school. He was three years her senior, but she'd skipped a grade in elementary school, so they weren't as far apart in grades as their ages inferred. She was a straight-A student and a gymnast. He played football; he might even have been the captain of the football team. He was good-looking and charming. Rebecca could see what initially drew her mother to him.

Ryan came from an interesting family. His father, Fred, was a hard-working miner, quiet and stubborn, who saved every penny he ever made. Her grandmother, Florence, was the life of the party, worked as a nurse's aide, and played a mean piano. Charlene and Ryan were opposite in so many ways, it left Rebecca questioning if that had played a role in the outcome of their family's lives. In her twenties, at a time when Rebecca went back to live with her, she learned that her grandmother was also an alcoholic, something that had been common knowledge to the rest of her family, but not to the younger grandchildren.

Rebecca wasn't clear what their living accommodations were like when her dad was growing up. She remembers in her younger years, going to visit her grandparents in an apartment they had beside the dairy. Rebecca vaguely recalled overhearing they had free rent because her grandmother nursed the founder of the dairy into his old age, an ancient old man who also lived there with them. The house that her grandparents had finally purchased in their seventies was quite possibly the very first house they ever owned. Her dad was the youngest of three in this very blue-collar family.

Charlene's parents, on the other hand, were as white-collar as they could be. Her grandfather, Frank, was an insurance guy and a banker. At one point, he owned six branches, which were bought out by a larger company and ultimately merged with a well-known global bank. In the early '70s, he built the first indoor mall in their town which still stands to this day. Some of her earliest memories of her maternal grandmother, Mildred, were of her owning an arts and crafts shop in that mall with her sister.

Growing up, Charlene had lived in a large five-level house on a sought-after court, enjoying luxuries at the hands of her father's success. He, too, battled with alcoholism and from what Rebecca learned after his passing, had been periodically abusive to his children. It is her thought that the lack of love Charlene felt from her own father is what drew her, at such a young age, to loving a boy who filled that emotional void.

When Charlene was eighteen years old, she and Ryan found themselves pregnant with Rebecca. As was deemed proper in those days, her parents married in front of a small number of guests in a dress Charlene had handmade for herself. Rebecca was due to be born on Halloween that fall, October 31.

Near the end of summer, her parents had decided to celebrate with a long weekend trip to the big city, eight hours away. At the time, her mom was seven months pregnant. While away, Charlene unexpectedly went into early labor. Their tumultuous life as a family began two months sooner than anticipated.

Rebecca remains uncertain of what happened between her birth and her parents' official separation almost six years later. No one ever talks about it and she can't say that she blames them.

They say our earliest memories begin to form around the age of three and a half and that girls tend to start remembering earlier than boys. As such, Rebecca was able to share with me memories dating back early on in her life.

She had been told that her parents' troubles started almost immediately. When Rebecca was just an infant, Charlene moved four hours away for a year of teacher's college. That's when Ryan realized caring for a small child was too much for him alone, and he enlisted the help of his older sister, Shirley. According to Aunt Shirley, Rebecca went to live with their family during that time, a fact strongly denied by Charlene.

Although Rebecca's recollection is foggy, she fondly remembers a few snapshots in time. Her aunt enrolled her in skating lessons just like her older cousin, Katherine. There was a skating carnival at the arena where her Uncle Henry coached the junior boy's hockey team that both of her cousins played for. She was only about one and a half years old, but vividly remembers being on the ice in front of a large crowd, presented with a small purple toy carpet sweeper. And, Rebecca felt loved, adored and wanted in their presence. She still does to this day.

As our conversations continued, Rebecca described for me the small wartime house the three of them moved into as a family. At that point, Ryan and Charlene were giving their marriage another shot. Rebecca was still very young, just two or three years old. Walking up the front steps, the entry door opened into the kitchen on the main floor. To the right was the living room with a big picture window looking out to the street. Behind the living room at the back right of the house was her parents' bedroom. A hallway ran down the middle to the back, with the bathroom on the left. Turning right, you found yourself at the bottom of the staircase leading up. At the top of the stairs, you could only go left or right. A spare bedroom on the right housed a guest bed and her mom's sewing machine. Her bedroom was on the left, with both bedrooms having very slanted roofs, being at the top of a house with no attic. She distinctly remembered her bedroom wallpaper with large purple flowers. She thinks perhaps their soothing hue is the source of her borderline infatuation with the color purple all her life. She felt safety in her room, an escape from the chaos. Those flowers were her friends and confidants.

As far back as her memory goes, she remembers waking often to the sounds of her parents arguing. It was a constant. She recalls specifically one night when she was about four years old, going downstairs asking them to please stop fighting so she could sleep.

Down the street from their house was a creek that their street was built over. In the winter, they would toboggan down the frozen creek bed for hours on end. She wouldn't have been much older than five and her parents allowed her to go there by herself any time she wanted. Where they lived in the north, winter usually stretched from early November to late April.

One day while tobogganing, Rebecca's mitt came off. It was a heavy-duty skidooing mitt that went almost to her elbow. She couldn't get it back on herself, and even though other kids offered, she'd only wanted her mom's help. She told her friends she'd be right back and asked them to keep an eye on her sled.

Off she went home to have her mom put her mitt back on. When she returned to the hill, it was completely deserted by the ten or more kids who had been there just ten minutes prior. Her toboggan was also nowhere to be found. She ran home as fast as she could to tell her parents. They put on their coats and together they trudged back to the hill. They were all searching for her sled when she saw her dad crawl into the culvert that went under the road. That section of the creek was protected from snowfall, so it was clear ice. She still remembers hoping her dad wouldn't fall through. He had spotted her toboggan deep in the depths of the tunnel and rescued it for her. It is one of very few memories Rebecca has of her parents together.

Other memories from her childhood still make her smile. The local convenience store was situated across from where they used to toboggan. One day, her parents gave her $5 to buy milk. They watched her cross the street in front of their house, as the store was on the opposite side of the road. Walking towards the store and out of sight of her parents, a teenage boy approached Rebecca eyeing the $5 bill she gripped in her hand. "Is that a five-dollar bill you have in your hand?" he inquired to which she proudly replied, "Yes! I'm going to buy milk." He asked if he could see the bill. Money was still very fascinating to her young mind and she could tell he shared the same appreciation, so she handed him the bill. But, next thing she knew, he was sprinting away with the milk money clenched tightly in his hand.

She ran back across the road, hollering for her dad to come quick. They jumped in his truck and drove in the direction the thief had fled. A few blocks down the road was another corner store. They surmised that if this thief was going to make quick work of his haul, he might have stopped there. When they entered the store, Rebecca spotted the boy immediately. As her dad approached him, he knew he'd been caught red-handed, as he saw Rebecca peeking out from behind the strange man. He returned the money, they bought milk and headed for home. Her dad was her hero that day.

It is obvious to Rebecca now, how her parents' absorption in their own lives forced her to become a terribly independent little girl. This was very apparent on Rebecca's first day of kindergarten. She put on her new blue dress with white collar and pleated skirt chosen especially for that day. She happily brushed her teeth and grabbed her bag and said goodbye to her mom, who said, "Wait a minute, I have to come with you." Rebecca looked at her in surprise and said, "Why? It's only around the corner and I know the way." "I have to take you to meet your teacher," her mother said. As they approached the gate leading into the schoolyard, Rebecca told her mom she could take it from there. Undeterred, her mother walked her all the way to her classroom and said hello to her teacher.

That same school year, she met the newest addition to their family. One February day, her parents returned home from the hospital with her new baby brother, Steven. Rebecca didn't remember her mom being pregnant or any conversations around having a new sibling, not to say they didn't happen. She does remember that shortly after coming home, her mom was about to bathe Steven in a baby bathtub on top of the kitchen table. Rebecca pulled up a chair in excitement to watch. But her delight turned quickly to shock as the warmth registered on her face. Her first memory of her brother was him peeing in her face.

One of the final memories Rebecca recalls from that house is a painful one. She was across the street helping the neighbors in their driveway. They'd taken a sledgehammer to their basement floor, which was full of cracks and needed replacing. The adults in the basement were filling four-quart baskets with the broken pieces of concrete, then passing them through the window to where the kids were standing in the driveway. The kids were then responsible for taking the concrete chunks and throwing them into the back of the pickup truck parked there. Once emptied, they'd pass the empty baskets back down through the window to be refilled again. Rebecca was standing with her friend, a boy her age, and his older brother who were all heavily engrossed in conversation. They were so absorbed that her friend picked up a piece of concrete and instead of throwing it into the truck, mistakenly threw it at Rebecca at close range.

That chunk hit her within millimeters of her right eye, blood pouring down her face immediately. She remembered the look of realization on her friend's face and how quickly she saw it flash from shock to apology and an immediate request for forgiveness. Rebecca ran across the street to her house where both her parents were home. They cleaned up the blood, inspected the cut, applied a butterfly bandage, and sent her on her way. She has the scar to this day, discreetly hidden in her laugh lines now more than ever.

The next memory stamped on her brain is the day they moved. She shook her head as she quietly described waking up to find all the family's belongings in boxes and laundry baskets, stacked on the front lawn. She asked her mom what was going on and was told they were moving, that her mom and dad didn't want to be married anymore. And, most shocking of all, that they, she and Steven and her mom, were moving 125 miles away to live with Len.

Growing up in that next house is a time in her life that Rebecca would prefer to forget.

When they arrived in Len's hometown, Rebecca learned that Charlene and Len had already purchased a home where they were all expected to live together. Len owned an older model two-door convertible sports car which would be their only family car for a few years. He put it away in the winter so the body wouldn't rust. So, for about six months of each year, they didn't have a vehicle. They would borrow Len's parents' car once a week to get groceries. Anything else they did on foot. Rebecca started piano lessons and was in the choir. She remembers walking everywhere in the freezing cold, always hoping a neighbor or someone she knew would offer her a ride. Len would catch a ride to work with a colleague and she and her mom would walk together to school and work, diverging at the bottom of the bridge each morning.

Soon after they moved, they discussed the semantics of how she would get back to see her dad. Rebecca missed him terribly. As part of the divorce settlement, her mom got sole custody of her while her dad got visitation when it was convenient. He also agreed to pay $50 a month to her mom until Rebecca turned sixteen. Things were very different back then. She remembered her mom saying once that she really didn't want his handouts, but, being the generous soul he was, he insisted she take something. But, if the post-dated checks for the year hadn't arrived, Rebecca's mom would have her following up with her dad directly. It was awkward to ask her dad for money and Rebecca wondered why her mother put her in that position.

In order to visit her dad, it was decided that, on a pre-arranged Friday night, she would board a Greyhound bus alone for the three-hour bus ride. They made sure she got the first seat close to the front and introduced her to the bus driver each time. She was five years old, traveling by herself to visit her dad. There was a rest stop along the way where she'd get off and buy herself a treat. And her dad would always be waiting for her at the station when she arrived to spend the weekend with him. He'd put her back on the bus on Sunday night, making it a late night going to bed once she arrived home.

As she shared this next story with me, I saw a flicker of hurt in her eyes. Rebecca talked about walking to school one morning, part way as usual with her mom. She was a fast walker, so you had to take big strides to keep up. It was after they'd lived in their new house for a few months. As Rebecca kept pace, Charlene asked her how she liked living there so far. With childlike naivete, she told her it was nice but that she wished they still lived with her Dad. Her mother stopped abruptly and said "You little bitch! We've tried so hard to make this a nice place for you and that's all you have to say?" Then her mother stormed off, telling her not to follow.

A few months later, Rebecca and her mother shared another memorable conversation, one that Rebecca says she will never forget. Charlene took her aside and said, "I think it's about time that you start calling Len, 'Dad'. That would make him feel a lot better and make us feel more like a family." Rebecca's mind raced. She ALREADY HAD A DAD. Why was it her job to make the adults feel better about themselves? It was an awful idea to her. But every time she used his given name, Len, she would get what she described as "the hairy eyeball" from her mom and quickly stammer a correction. Rebecca learned it was easier just to call him Dad, to appease both of them and to have one less reason to set off his short fuse. Rebecca admitted that, in those times, she also felt more like a human being to Len instead of the nuisance she was typically reduced to.

After a few months of calling Len, Dad, her mom decided it was time for another conversation. To aid in the appearance of them being a family, her mother suggested that Rebecca change her last name to Len's. In reflection, she has no idea where, at the tender age of six, she had the wherewithal to tell her mom she needed time to think about it. But she immediately knew her answer. She already had a dad and he was still very much alive and part of her life. What would he think, and how would he feel if she changed her name? Rebecca knew it would make him incredibly sad. She readdressed the topic with her mom the next day, telling her that she'd decided to keep her own last name. She doesn't think the decision ever sat well with her mom. She knows that hearing her last name was a constant reminder of the past her mom was trying to put behind her. To this day, Rebecca continues to actualize the ramifications of that choice. The full impact could never have been predicted.

At Christmas, they'd receive cards addressed to the family's last name. Rebecca knows that no one intentionally left her out, but already feeling like an outsider in this family, each year those cards nudged her even more. She acknowledged these are things many blended families deal with, but combined with the acrimony she already felt from her parents, not feeling part of the family became commonplace.

Fast forward a few years and by the age of 12, Rebecca's hair had grown fairly long. On one particular weekend visit, her Dad suggested that it might be nice for her to get a haircut and her ears pierced. That was a taboo subject. She'd been asking Len and Charlene to get her ears pierced for a few years, but their answer had always been that she had to wait until she was 16. Their reasoning was if she was allergic to cheap metals and could only wear real gold or silver, she would have to be old enough to get a job to pay for her own earrings.

She reminded her Dad of their refusal but he said he'd take care of it. So off they went to see a hairdresser friend of his, to cut a substantial amount of her hair to chin length. And then they got her ears pierced. She felt like a queen. Not only did she have a new hairstyle, she had bright, shiny gold studs in her ears, something she'd wanted for so long. She was on cloud nine when Ryan called Charlene to let her know. During that conversation, he used the unfortunate term "ravishing" to describe his daughter's new look. Charlene was irate and asked Ryan why on earth it would be appropriate for a 12-year-old to look ravishing. It was a short and heated conversation that completely burst Rebecca's bubble.

The three-hour bus ride home that Sunday night was the longest one Rebecca had experienced. She dreaded seeing them at the bus station. She was wearing a toque and was told to leave it on, even after they'd arrived home. She recounted to me how she was sitting on her bed in her room, unpacking her things from the weekend, when Charlene came in. Without saying a word, she took one look at her ears, shook her head and wrenched the earrings off. To anyone who has not been exposed to newly pierced ears, during the early stages of the healing process, the ears are tender and there is substantial fluid excreted that dries around the stud. You are instructed to spin the studs often, so the earrings don't stick in place. And, the back of new piercing studs is clasped on extra tightly to ensure that it doesn't fall off during the first six weeks. Rebecca remembers feeling shocked by how she was treated; that a mom could exhibit such hatred towards her child, both physically and emotionally. She knows that much of her mom's anger was directed towards her ex-husband, Ryan, but he wasn't in proximity, so she was the easiest target. On top of the intense pain, it also made her feel very sad, alone, and afraid.

What stemmed from that incident proved how intentional Rebecca has been in her actions from a very early age. When Rebecca turned 16, Charlene proudly stated that she was now old enough to get her ears pierced and asked when she could take her. Rebecca was very matter of fact in stating that she had promised her father that when she was finally allowed to get her ears pierced, she would let him do the honors during her next visit with him. Rebecca was surprised when Charlene exhibited

52

enough self-control to hold back the biting comment she knew was on the tip of her tongue.

As I looked back on all the stories that Rebecca had shared with me up to this point in her young life, I was a little humbled by all that she'd endured. As she had only provided me with anecdotal snippets of what she experienced, I was hopeful that her next stories would paint a different picture.

CHAPTER 5

Nicole (Part 1): We Are Family

Nicole is one of those people blessed with a photographic memory. She described to me what had transpired that *year*, in such vivid detail, I almost felt like I had been there in person.

One of the reasons Nicole believed she had been identified as a good resource to work on the family reunion project was because she had spent nine summers in a row at the venue they had selected. She'd started out as a camper, progressed to camp counselor and their extended family would rent it the last weekend of each summer. They were hoping to hold the reunion in August.

She had begun looking into renting the camp for the family more than a year and a half before it came to fruition. She heard the property might be going up for sale so the first thing she did was confirm they could still rent. From there, she needed to determine which weeks were available and what worked for their families, as many would be making the trek from quite a distance.

It was a ton of work coordinating back and forth. There were deposits to make and contracts to sign. There was a need for an additional, separate insurance policy that wound up costing far more than expected. In May, Anna, one of Nicole's cousins offered to assist with the reunion plans. Nicole will forever be grateful for everything she did to ensure they had a fabulous week. From planning a scavenger hunt to their Talent Show, outdoor games for the kids to play, organizing enough board games to keep them occupied in case of bad weather, Anna was on it. They talked about meal options and who would do what. She created a Facebook page where they could keep everyone up to date and answer all sorts of questions. It was a time when Nicole so enjoyed working and planning with someone who was so like-minded.

Leading up to the date, there were many decisions to make and tasks to coordinate. Nicole's brother, Craig, and sister-in-law, Carole, couldn't make it due to work commitments, but they really wanted their kids to be able to enjoy the reunion with their cousins. So, her brother flew them in for two of the most fun and incredible weeks Nicole and her family had ever spent with them.

With Nicole and her husband, Rob, going to Camp with five kids in tow, Craig's three and their two, they knew they were taking on a huge responsibility. But they were up for it. They arranged sleeping bags and pillows and all things necessary for her nieces and nephew to enjoy their week, short of the suitcases they would be bringing with them. They would be responsible for the five oldest grandchildren going to the reunion. One of the things Nicole had anticipated as a possible issue was their habit of sleeping in, as teenagers are prone to do. And if that happened, they would potentially miss the 9:30 am cut off for Uncle Tom's Breakfast Bonanza each morning. Then they'd looking for food just before lunch, messing up their mealtimes and shifting their whole eating timetable. Nicole knew she had to ensure that didn't happen because it would affect everyone. She proposed an Arctic Wake-

Up Dip as a solution. Every morning by 8 am, they had to be down at the lake and in the water deep enough to dunk their whole body. Nicole promised there would be an awesome prize for those who did it all five mornings in a row. It was a huge success; they started with nineteen and ended the week with twelve of them having done the dip every single day. Their cabin woke up every morning at 7:45 am, threw on their bathing suits, grabbed a towel, stopped at the bathrooms on the way, then dunked in the lake - all seven of them did it for the entire five days. What started out as a ruse to get the kids up at a decent time turned into memories that will last their lifetime. Nicole was also thrilled to have avoided the adults' disdain, which had been her priority.

In the Facebook group, they were busily planning their schedules. It was decided that while Uncle Tom cooked daily breakfast for everyone, each family would be responsible for their own lunches. For dinner, they would have an online sign-up board where one large family or combined smaller groups would take on the task of feeding everyone for one night during the week. Nicole's cousins grabbed the first night they were arriving, Sunday, right away. Tom and Rose said they would put on a big turkey dinner on the Monday night, providing for lots of leftovers for the week. Nicole and Rob and the kids signed up for Tuesday night, proudly exclaiming that they would be hosting a Mexican Fiesta. They had so many ideas.

After their announcement on the sign-up board, it was asked what menu they had planned for Mexican Night. Nicole wrote that they'd do tacos and enchiladas and quesadillas and tortillas and salsa. Then a message popped up by one aunt, saying, "We don't do Mexican.

Can't do spices or peppers." Nicole replied saying they were feeding all palates, from kids to adults so while there might be some with some spices, those would be very mild. And there would be a variety to choose from. The taco bar would be a make-your-own, so they could select what to put in them. Nicole also suggested that if that didn't work, that there would likely be leftovers from the turkey dinner.

Nicole did not expect what happened next. She received a private message that said – "Nicole, I do not appreciate the response you gave on the Family Reunion site. Like it or not, we are still your Aunt and Uncle and deserve respect like all your other Aunts and Uncles. I have a sensitive stomach since the cancer. Telling me to eat left-overs is uncalled for and rude. Also, giving your uncle snide looks at your sister's wedding was also uncalled for, he has M.S. Have some respect."

Nicole provided me with some context. Her stepfather was George. George's youngest sister, Gladys, was only seven years older than Nicole. Gladys had always insisted that Nicole call her aunt, even when she was twelve years old and Nicole was five. Nicole wasn't sure of the last time she'd talked to them before that, it could have been over ten years. Nicole didn't have their address, nor was she even sure where they lived. And she never learned what was meant by the snide looks.

This same family member also questioned why Nicole was doing cabin assignments, why she was in charge. Gladys had not stepped up to help in any way but was certainly available in the background to throw shade. Nicole spent a few days thinking about how to respond. She envisioned Gladys sending bullets back and the conversation never ending. Ultimately, Nicole decided to call George about it, since she was his sister. He could deal with it.

They also learned that Gladys and her husband, Hank, and their son, Victor, would have to leave the reunion early for a doctor's appointment. They had signed up to feed everyone on Thursday night and now had to leave before dinner on Wednesday. Instead of trading nights with someone, they simply posted a note on the board indicating that their Thursday dinner time slot was vacant.

In the meantime, George called Nicole and told her about the discussion he had with two of his siblings about Gladys. Apparently, more than one of the cousins had been on the receiving end of her diatribes. They suggested the easiest way to rectify the dinner situation would be for Nicole to move her dinner to a night once Gladys and Hank were gone. That was something that Nicole had already run by Anna as an option. Unfortunately, with this aunt being the youngest child, she had been pandered to her whole life and expected to get her own way, especially when it involved family. Nicole told George she had no issue with moving her night. She only wanted him to know that she felt they were enabling Gladys' never-ending demands and sense of entitlement, which she didn't think was right or productive. Regardless, he agreed and appreciated Nicole moving her night.

Going back to the planning for the week, arrival time was set for midday on Sunday. Nicole and Rob's son, Nate's baseball team had been entered into a tournament at the last minute the weekend they were to arrive. Since George's sister, Edna, lived the closest to the camp, Nicole had asked if she would consider doing the walkthrough with the Camp Representative on the Sunday they arrived. That way, she would learn how everything worked and what their responsibilities would be as it pertained to garbage, recycling, clean-up, etc. It would also entail being there the following Saturday to walk through a camp check with the same person, ensuring they were leaving it in the same condition they'd found it. Edna said she had no problem being that person and Nicole appreciated it greatly, as she had no idea what time they'd be arriving. They also weren't sure when they'd be leaving as Nicole's daughter, Zoe, had a ball tournament at the end of the week they needed to back down south for. The schedule had yet to be posted.

Rob and Nicole took two separate vehicles because there were seven of them along with all their luggage and camp necessities. Rob and Zoe were probably leaving Friday and Nate was considering going with them as he usually helped Rob coach Zoe's team. Nicole was still undecided as to when she'd leave with Craig's kids. She thought she would play that by ear.

Because of the unknown timeline for Nate's ball tournament they were also unsure of when they'd arrive at Camp. The team would simply play until they lost out. In the meantime, Nicole and her brother, Craig, arranged for the arrival of his kids. There had been discussion about them spending some time with their grandparents, George and Sandra, once they arrived at Nicole's, before going up to Camp. There were a lot of moving pieces to coordinate as George had some appointments that he was still waiting to confirm. Once the kids had settled in at Nicole's, and George and Sandra had firmed up their schedule, it was decided that Nicole and the kids would meet them halfway at lunchtime on the Friday before Camp. Craig's kids would go to Nana Sandra and Papa George's house for two days for a visit and based on how well Nate's team did, they would then determine how everyone would get to Camp on Sunday.

Nate's ball team had a dismal record for the season but surprisingly made it into the finals on Sunday afternoon. So, George and Sandra went ahead to Camp with Craig's kids. Nicole and Rob, Nate and Zoe, didn't arrive until 9:30 that night.

Once they got settled in, they had a chance to chat with Craig's kids about their time with Nana Sandra and Papa George. Nicole remembers feeling sad about their drive up to Camp. Nana had rented kayaks and paddleboards which were strapped to the top of their car. The three kids were forced to sit silently in the back seat for the three-and-a-half-hour drive. They weren't allowed to talk loudly or listen to the radio. They had to listen for any change in the sound of the items strapped to the car. Jade, the oldest granddaughter, told Nicole that her phone had died twenty minutes into the ride, so the following three hours had been horrendous. Nicole felt so disappointed for them and was determined to make up for it during the week. And, she did.

Nicole remembers getting the cabin set up. Each of them had their own space. They hung a clothesline for wet bathing suits and towels which led to a clothespin fight one night where they whipped them at each other, dissolving into giggles. There were seven of them and Nicole knew they'd have to work hard to ensure the cabin didn't become a pigsty. Every morning after breakfast, each one of the kids took a turn sweeping out the cabin, five mornings and five kids. It worked well and kept the cabin tidy for the week.

They shared so much laughter that week inside their little cabin of seven. In discussion with Nicole, she told me it felt as though she had compartmentalized Camp into two separate memories - the good ones and the bad ones.

There were many good memories like the Scavenger Hunt and Talent Show, the Arctic Dip and delicious meals, a group hike, and the campfires. Nicole's cousins owned a bouncy castle company and brought one that even the adults could jump in. That was a big hit. Nicole undeniably has warm, grateful memories from Camp.

One good memory that still makes her laugh took place when a bunch of them were in front of the main lodge. Her Aunt Rose was there along with a few of the cousins. Something was said, and Nicole exclaimed, "everyone knows I'm your favorite, Auntie Rose." The look on Rose's face was priceless. She is the kind of person who never wants anyone to feel left out or have their feelings hurt, but secretly she knew what Nicole was saying was the truth. Her face flashed between acknowledgment of the truth and compassion for the other cousins. The recollection dissolved Nicole into giggles again.

And then there were the bad memories that had begun even before they arrived. The message Nicole received about their Mexican dinner menu being too spicy might have been a foreshadowing. Ultimately, it was the ongoing tension with her sister, Sheila, and her ever-present sense of entitlement that proved to be the biggest catalyst that week. It emerged as a shared family trait for the youngest daughters.

Leading up to Camp, Craig and his wife, Carole, talked to Nicole about their kids. They wanted to ensure that they wouldn't be made to feel obligated to watch Sheila's kids, a common occurrence. Mackenzie, Sheila's oldest, was three while Martin would turn two that fall.

Craig asked Nicole to manage that situation closely, so they weren't taken advantage of. Everyone agreed, this was their vacation too. Nicole had promised she'd keep a close watch.

Nicole had planned a ten-minute morning workout at 10 am every day in front of the main lodge, where she would lead the exercises. Tuesday morning, Sandra was participating when Craig's middle daughter, Jordan, walked up wearing her bathing suit. Nicole's mom asked if she was wearing sunscreen. Jordan said she wasn't. Sandra insisted she go put on a t-shirt right away or get some sunscreen on. At this point, they were halfway through the ten-minute workout. Jordan is also not a fair-skinned girl, so five minutes would not have made a difference. Jordan asked for permission to finish the exercises first, but Sandra looked at her incredulously and said, "No, go do it now." If Nicole hadn't been leading the exercises, she would have suggested her mom be a little more reasonable, but that didn't happen.

That afternoon, Nicole's Aunt Edna (George's oldest sister) approached her hoping for a conversation, which they had in the back room off the kitchen. Edna told her that she had witnessed an incident between Sheila and Jordan and that she had stopped Sheila from going any further. Sheila's daughter, Mackenzie, had taken off again, something that had already happened a few times when she was left unattended by her mom. The camp is set on a large lake, easily accessible for even small children. Sheila had been looking frantically for Mackenzie when she came upon Jordan and Mackenzie leaving the bathrooms. Edna told her that Sheila lit into Jordan, telling her that she needed to tell someone when she had Mackenzie and that what she had done was unacceptable. Jordan started to explain that Mackenzie came up to her and said she had to go to the bathroom, so Jordan took her. Sheila didn't accept her explanation and told her she should never do that without telling someone. That's when Edna stepped in and told Sheila that Jordan was only trying to help and that there was no reason that she should be getting in trouble. Edna said Sheila finally stopped yelling at Jordan at that point and they went their separate ways.

After Nicole had witnessed the sunscreen incident and then heard about the Mackenzie situation, she took Jordan aside, gave her a warm hug, told her she loved her and that she was sorry people were coming down on her. Nicole told Jordan that she knew it was difficult to go two weeks without her parents, and that she hoped she and Rob were people she felt she could come to for a hug when she needed it. Nicole felt so much love for her in that moment. It had been a taxing day all around so that night, they decided to call Craig and Carole.

Craig and Nicole spent a few minutes talking about how much Sheila was having his kids look after her kids. Craig said he wished he was there so he could put an immediate stop to it. In that moment Nicole felt like she was doing his kids a disservice, so she vowed to be more vigilant about their interactions with Mackenzie and Martin.

Part of the problem was Sheila's husband, Shane. As an avid outdoorsman, he and George had secured the use of a motorboat for the week, so he could fish. When they woke up in the morning, he was gone. When he came back at night, he usually went right back to their cabin. Nicole couldn't remember speaking to him more than once or twice that entire week. Nicole assumed that put a lot of pressure on Sheila to look after her kids on her own all the time. What surprised her the most was the expectation Sheila had of others to help her with her kids in her husband's absence. They had expected a few requests, but it was getting ridiculous. Many times, Nicole found the three oldest girls, Jade, Jordan, and Zoe, looking after Sheila's two kids. On Tuesday night, Rob, George, and Nicole were playing crib. Sheila walked by and said to George, "When you're done that hand, can you go put Martin to bed?" Nicole knows George saw her eyes bug out of her head when Sheila said that. But, after the hand was done, George got up and did it. Earlier in the day, Sheila needed Sandra's phone to use as a monitor to watch Martin while he was sleeping. Sandra is a real estate agent and was waiting on some time-sensitive information to get to a client. Sheila kept texting her asking when she was bringing her phone and to hurry up. Sandra had a look of exasperation on her face, trying to juggle the needs of her client against the demands of her daughter. Nicole knew it was best for her not to say a word.

As I sat in awe of Nicole's self-discipline, she glanced down at her phone. She realized she'd been talking straight for one full hour and still had so much more to share. She hadn't really gotten to the good parts yet. She promised me she'd remember exactly where she left off to ensure she picked right back up the next time.

CHAPTER 6

Julie: Cake for Breakfast?

My conversations with Julie that *year* were centered around the great relationships she had enjoyed with her grandparents while growing up. They were a staple around holidays, for sure, but it was more than that. They had made her feel special for being herself, the whole year through. One of her grandfathers affectionately called her "Brat", a term that leaves her smiling with fond memories when she hears it, even today.

Julie lovingly recalled lazy summer days spent at her grandparents' cottage as a kid, learning to waterski off their dock. She collected old pennies with her grandfather and got paid one dollar for each one she found that was minted before she was born. It was such a treat when her other grandmother always put everything aside upon learning that her granddaughter was coming to visit, to ensure a quart of chocolate milk was in the fridge, chilled for her arrival. Julie also had the great fortune of stopping at her grandparents on the way home from school each night to practice piano. A bittersweet memory she revealed to me was when her grandfather, sick with cancer, gave her money for university. He had been saving it for one final trip home but knew he would never make it.

It was because of these wonderful bonds, and all the great experiences she shared with her grandparents as a child, that she was excited to see her children develop the same kinds of relationships with their grandparents.

As her kids got older and became teenagers, Julie couldn't help but notice a shift in their moods after they'd return from a visit with one set of their grandparents. She knew they had grown to an age where they knew right from wrong, self-aware enough to identify when a situation made them feel uncomfortable or awkward. Julie didn't want to unnecessarily stir any pots, but couldn't quiet the nagging voice in her head. As a parent, she felt it incumbent upon her to learn more about the time her kids were spending with their grandparents. She carefully planned what she would say and what questions she would ask about their visits.

As it turned out, Julie was right to be concerned. Upon speaking with each of her children separately, she learned that they were, in fact, uncomfortable being guests in their grandparents' home. They were regularly scolded for having bad table manners by their grandfather, bad manners that included such grievous affronts as, after cutting their food, not switching the fork to their right hand to take a bite.

The visits were tense away from the dinner table as well. Her kids admitted to feeling immense relief when it was time to come home, glad to finally be out of the strict household their mother had been raised in. Where it had once been a treat to visit with their grandparents, Julie learned these visits were something her kids were becoming desperate to avoid.

Julie told me about a particularly unsettling story that she felt had forced her hand into taking action. She and her family were invited to a week of skiing in the mountains with her parents, siblings, and their families; two condos would provide lodging for the occasion. They politely declined for two reasons. The first was simple: Julie preferred the warmth, and the thought of spending money on a winter ski vacation made her shudder. The second reason could be summed up as self-preservation. With all those people together for a week, sharing two condominiums, chaos seemed inevitable, harsh words and judgments likely, and tears a genuine risk. Julie had wanted no part.

Even though Julie and her husband declined the invitation, her parents pushed to have the kids join them on the trip. During a family discussion, the kids took many factors into consideration. It was decided that they could miss a week of school if it was something they really wanted to do. Before they left, Julie and her husband talked to their children at length and took extra care to make sure they were comfortable with the arrangements.

While their grandparents could be challenging, her kids adored their cousins, and they were especially looking forward to spending quality time with them. Before she'd agreed to send them on the trip, Julie had spoken with her brother, Dean, and his wife, Lynn, and they'd agreed to act as surrogate parents during the week, lending a hand or a hug as needed. Julie had no worries that they would be a great buffer for the kids and that they'd be in good hands with their aunt and uncle. Thanks to this planning, the only time they'd be alone with their grandparents would be while traveling to and from the airport, and Julie was confident that her kids could manage that.

Throughout the week, Julie received updates from her brother and her sister-in-law. The week had started off nicely. Julie's sister, Leanne, got engaged, which was cause for celebration. In fact, it seemed like the family's vacation was going very well... until it wasn't.

Julie's mother had taken a "day off" to babysit Leanne's two young children, so Leanne could go skiing instead. Things changed quickly after Julie's father fell on the hill and dislocated his shoulder. He returned to the condo before heading to the hospital, and his arrival ushered in a sense of panic. Dean and Lynn were called in from the slopes to provide extra hands on deck, and Leanne made her way back as soon as she heard. The minute Leanne returned, Julie's mother was ready to hand off the baby to her, so she could attend to her injured husband. But, upon entering the condo, Leanne turned towards her bedroom because apparently, it was imperative that she change out of her ski clothes before retrieving her child.

According to her brother's retelling, Julie said this is when things really started to unravel. Instead of chasing after Leanne, Julie's mother set the baby down so that she could take care of her husband. The baby started to cry, not surprisingly. Leanne rarely put him down, reacting to his every need, so this was a foreign circumstance to him. The rising tension and anxiety the adults in the condo were feeling would have upset anyone. Leanne, re-materializing almost immediately at the sound was quick to criticize her mother for ignoring her grandson's cries. Dean swears that she had even ordered their mom to pick the baby back up, before disappearing into her room (childless) once again and taking the time to change out of her ski clothes completely before she resurfaced.

70

It seemed that Leanne's actions were the family's last straw, a tipping point for the overt display of anger that ensued. Dean had readily admitted that he was fuming and that he let his words fly. Julie chose to spare me the profane details of what was actually said, and she was thankful that the older kids knew enough to flee the scene, retreating to the other condo as the situation escalated. That was all it took. The week was in ruins, and the vacation never recovered.

As the week finally came to a close, Julie's father was still on light medication to manage his pain. Still, he had been cleared to drive, so they packed Julie's kids and their belongings into his vehicle. The trip from the condo to the city was three-and-a-half hours, and according to her kids, time seemed to slow down from the moment they departed. They were seated in the back, with their grandparents in the front, and for over three hours, they listened to them bicker and fight about everything, from his driving abilities to the sounds her grandmother inadvertently made when she breathed.

Julie felt for her kids. It wasn't hard for her to empathize with them, recalling the agony of her own childhood car rides. She knew what it had been like for her younger self sharing such close space with her parents and siblings. She remembered well how she would listen to her parents' incessant bickering from the back seat, and wishing desperately that she could teleport... to anywhere but there.

Dean's birthday fell on the last day of the trip, and the family had planned to celebrate with dinner in the city, before returning to their respective night's accommodations. But, by the time they arrived in the city, Julie's father was in a stormy mood and stubbornly refused to join them. Dean, wondering if he'd done something wrong, went to talk to his father but his dad refused to engage. He pushed a bit further telling his dad he'd like to have a conversation like two adults, after all their dad would be getting on a plane the following day and who knows what could happen. Apparently unmoved by that possibility, their father told him "Some things are just better left unsaid."

Dean celebrated his birthday with his family that night, going out to dinner just like they had planned - with one exception. Selfishly, their father chose to dine on fast food, walking alone to Burger King instead of spending the evening in celebration of his son.

Julie was waiting for her kids at the airport when they returned with their grandparents. They decided to all grab lunch together before her parents left to make their drive home. Once they were done eating, Julie piled her kids' luggage into her truck, and everyone said their goodbyes and thank-yous. Her son, apparently happy to be home, was quick to strap himself into the passenger seat as he pulled the door shut behind him. After he released the biggest sigh she'd ever heard from him, he simply said "Oh my gawd, I'm glad that's over." Hearing assent from the back seat, her kids were recast from rivals into allies, united in surviving the stress of the vacation they'd just returned from.

On the drive home, Julie tried to be there for her kids. She asked them questions and listened to them speak, knowing they probably had a lot to share about the week they'd just experienced. She could imagine how they felt and had trouble shaking off her own guilt for putting them in the situation. Although they had loved the skiing and time with their cousins, the negative undertone of the conversation did not go unnoticed.

Upon returning home, the kids quickly settled back into routine. Julie was glad her kids were so resilient, proud of them actually. But there was a guilt that continued to gnaw at her until she could ignore it no longer, prompting our conversation.

As she sat in my office, the immense conflict she felt was staring me in the face. On one hand, she longed for her kids to experience the incredible grandparent bond that she fondly remembered. Weren't kids' visits with their grandparents supposed to be punctuated with cake for breakfast and ignored bedtimes? On the other hand, the toxicity that they were being exposed to could have lasting effects, that she knew too well.

I asked Julie if she'd ever tried to talk to her parents about their approach, both with her and her kids. She assured me, she had tried every avenue possible to bridge the gap in their perceptions. Each time, it had been like banging her head against a brick wall, with a finger always pointed back at her as the one who required a readjustment.

Her decision felt like a lose-lose situation. If she left things the way they were, she sensed she was putting her kids in the line of fire. Julie all too easily remembered the stabbing pain of their authoritarian approach and offhand remarks, cutting to the core. If her kids experienced even one iota of that, it was too much for her. Their involuntary proximity to the obliviously selfish behavior of her parents wasn't fair.

On the other hand, if she limited her kids' time with her parents, their future relationship may be hampered. Perhaps visits in the future could be better, especially as they grew to adults. Was she in charge of potentially taking that opportunity away from all of them? It wasn't lost on her that her parents would most likely be incredibly hurt by the noticeable absence of her kids in their lives. She also acknowledged the scorn she would be sure to receive as the perceived driver of the separation.

As we talked through her options, a confidence in her resolve had begun to appear on her face. Acknowledging the factors that were most important to her, she talked through the impact that each option would have on her kids.

Her own childhood was history, set firmly in the past. Nothing could be done about that. What she could do something about, what she felt she had to do something about, was protecting her children, and their childhood memories, from the damage their callous, self-absorbed grandparents could do.

CHAPTER 7

Christine (Part 1): A Welcome Addition?

Christine had just completed third grade when Patricia and Larry, her mom and stepfather, informed her and her younger brother, Todd, that they were expecting a new addition to the family. She remembered the mixed emotions she felt at the news. On one hand, it would be exciting and fun to have a new baby in the house, but on the other hand, her Spidey-senses were tingling. She had felt deep down that there would be something wrong with this baby. She couldn't explain to me why.

When the time came to meet Samantha, Christine was relieved to see that she looked 'normal'. Aside from the small marks behind each of her ears from the forceps, she was rosy and healthy. Christine's pent-up worry relaxed. For some reason, she hadn't expected her to be born fully intact. She wasn't sure if she anticipated she'd be missing a limb or an organ. No matter the seemingly outside perfection of this baby, Christine still subconsciously harbored skepticism. Deep down, she questioned how two people, who didn't seem complete themselves, could create a whole human being just by coming together.

She didn't fault them for where they were in their lives. Her mom, Patricia, had been a teenage mother and had given up a lot to have her. She missed much of her youth and told Christine on one memorable occasion, that her life would have been very different if Christine had never been born.

Her biological parents did "the right thing" by getting married, but it didn't take long for their marriage to crumble. In telling the story, Christine mused that it couldn't have been easy for her mom, going from her parents' home, to wife and mother, to divorced and remarried all in a ten-year span.

Her stepfather, Larry, was three years younger than her mom. They were both saddled with big responsibilities at an incredibly young age. In retrospect, Christine didn't believe they had time to find themselves or each other as a couple as the burden of life and kids had always taken precedence.

After Samantha came home from the hospital, she slept in her crib in Larry and Patricia's room for the first while. Eventually, it was decided that the girls would share and leave Todd, the only boy, with his own room. Although it made perfect sense to her parents, sharing a room with someone ten years younger was even worse than it sounded. Samantha went to bed much earlier, requiring Christine to sneak into their pitch-black room each night to silently undress and fumble her way into bed. Their closet, dresser space, mirror space, you name it, all shared. The room wasn't very big, and Christine felt no privacy. They shared a room until she was almost seventeen. This, amongst other issues at home, weighed heavily on Christine and it was never her happy place.

Sitting in my office, she shivered slightly as she described typical winter mornings when Larry would make breakfast. Patricia was usually in the shower and the kids would be eating. He'd then go outside to scrape the ice off the windshield while warming up the van. Coming back inside, he'd make his way around the breakfast table to kiss them all goodbye sporting a wet, icy mustache. The recollection of those cold, gross, soggy goodbyes makes her shudder to this day.

And then there was the winter Samantha had whooping cough. She'd wake up coughing and coughing every night until she threw up. Christine wound up sleeping on the pullout couch in the basement until Samantha was better. She didn't fault her for being sick, she just wanted some sleep.

Christine felt then and still feels to this day, that Samantha was the golden child who could do no wrong. This was validated predominantly by the special treatment Samantha received, no matter how dreadful her behavior.

Christine divulged that many times, she and Todd got in trouble, while Samantha got off scot-free. Being the oldest, Christine was frequently told she should know better. It was an ongoing issue in their household, one that had her spending as little time there as possible. It wasn't worth it. When she was home, she was in trouble for something. It was simply easier not to be there.

As life went on and Christine finally escaped the confines of her upbringing, she realized that her early intuition had been right after all.

Years after Christine moved out, Samantha's behavior became increasingly erratic and unpredictable. Police presence was required on a few occasions involving physical altercations between Samantha and their parents. There was mention of hospital stays and in various wards, as they waited for a diagnosis. Christine doesn't know the specifics of what took place, nor will she ever. She surmised it was none of her business and preferred it that way.

Christine remembered Todd telling her a story about the time he got into a bar fight in his late teens. A beer bottle flew through the huge front window, smashing it into pieces. The finger was pointed at him. He had a court date but was told that if he paid for the repair in full, all charges would be dropped. Christine recalled it being a substantial amount of money at that time for a kid - about $1200. He told her he had worked and saved and kept his money hidden in his sock drawer. Not long before the court date, he wanted to confirm he'd saved enough. According to his mental calculations, he was close. But the sock was empty and he was in a panic.

Around the same time, Samantha arrived home with a brand-new stereo system. Back then, they came with a turntable and cassette deck and typically a mean set of speakers. She said she had been babysitting and saving birthday money for a while to afford it. But to Todd, it had seemed a large amount to have saved without ever talking to the rest of the family about it. It seemed too coincidental. Only a week until his court date and he had no money. Todd was in a bind.

Finally, he told Larry, adding that he suspected Samantha might have been responsible for the empty sock. It took Samantha almost a week to admit it had been her. Christine didn't know if it was a teenage mistake or relevant to her mental health diagnosis. But it made Christine question her interactions with Samantha, which were limited at best. They didn't get along. Should she have tried harder? Was she the big sister she should have been?

Sharing these musings with me late that year, much time had passed in between. She'd already had many years of contemplation. Christine had gone back and forth between her gut instinct that said their relationship would just never be, and Larry and Patricia's wishes to accept Samantha as she was and be the doting big sister they so desperately wanted her to be. Over the years, they'd provided her with literature and cd's about the disorder, hoping it would help her perceive Samantha in a more positive light.

Christine told me about a phone call she'd received from Samantha about ten years earlier. She had very specific questions about her life's timeline. How old had she been when she met Kevin, moved in with him, got engaged, married, bought a house, had each of her kids? Christine challenged her need to know, to which Samantha had responded, "Your life is so perfect, I want to do everything you did." Christine said she'd spent a lot of time making her life for her family as great as she knew how. She had learned what worked specifically for them and moved forward accordingly. She was emphatic in sharing that what she did was right for them but didn't guarantee success for anyone else. She encouraged Samantha to forge her own path.

Fast forward those ten years to Samantha's wedding, planned for spring break, in the mountains. The thought of spending a vacation in cold weather didn't thrill Christine. Their family was used to traveling to warm climates during winter and spring breaks, to get away from the cold. Since Kevin had started a new job the previous spring and his staff had already asked for the time off, they hadn't gone on their usual warm trip at Christmas.

She found it interesting that her brother, Todd, and his wife, Jessica, asked if their family was going to the wedding. If they didn't go, their absence would be duly noted. But they knew her disdain for anything cold and the fact that her relationship with Samantha was tenuous. There was no good way out of it. Besides, it gave her kids and their cousins, Todd and Jessica's kids, the chance to spend a week snowboarding together, which was a suitable trade-off.

A few months before the wedding day, she found herself on one of Samantha's impromptu and unexpected conference calls. Christine joined Samantha and her fiancé, Tim, on one line, and Todd on another. After a few pleasantries, they asked if she and Todd would be co-emcees for their wedding. Christine had never met Tim in person, but they had shared a few family facetime chats. Todd, on the other hand, had spent a lot of time with them, so it made sense to ask him. It was no secret that Todd was never extremely organized, a fact Christine was sure played into their decision. They were aware of her public speaking abilities, coupled with her organizational skills, so they really needed them both. It would be a good mix. As she and Todd were accepting and thanking them for the opportunity, Tim chimed in to say they'd asked his sister first, but she'd declined, citing her dislike for speaking in public. Samantha quickly spoke overtop of Tim, trying to recover from his unprompted, and supposedly secret admission.

Christine shared with me how she remembered feeling as the week of the wedding approached. She, Kevin and the kids were booked to fly out the Monday morning on an early flight. While checking in the day before, Christine had learned their flight had been canceled. Why hadn't they been notified? Was it a sign? Were they not supposed to go? She had immediately called the airline and after much negotiation, they were finally confirmed on a flight two hours later than their original booking. The next morning, they got to the airport in plenty of time to enjoy a nice breakfast. As they called for preboarding for those with young kids and in executive class, they didn't pay much attention. With seats close to the front, their rows were called next. As they boarded the plane, the kids walked in front, searching for their seats. As Christine rounded the corner and headed down the aisle, she heard a woman's voice inquire – Ryan? Emma? Turns out her parents, Patricia and Larry, were on the same flight, seated just two rows in front of them. They were all a bit shocked at the coincidence.

Christine then told me about a brush with fame that she knew had nothing to do with her story but thought it neat to share. Sitting in the row between them and her parents was country singer, Dallas Smith, and his wife, Kristen. He had just come off a Country Album of the Year win the night before at the Juno Awards. They wrote him a quick congratulatory note from the fans sitting behind him.

Once they arrived at the airport and were waiting at the carousel for their luggage, they discussed what they needed to do next. Something fun they did on trips was to have the kids lead the way through the airports. If one of them had guided them from their car to their gate at their home airport, then the other was responsible for getting them from the plane to whatever form of transportation they were taking on the other end. On that trip, they were renting a minivan to easily fit the four of them, all the luggage, and snowboarding equipment. It was affordable and fit their needs. Christine sheepishly admitted that she had owned a minivan for "five long years" when her kids were young. She told me she had done her "minivan penance" and hadn't planned to drive one ever again but was willing to for one week.

Christine's parents joined them at the luggage carousel. Larry got restless and went to see about their car rental, leaving Patricia to collect their luggage on her own.

Once the luggage arrived, the child responsible for directing them at that airport, successfully led them to the car rental desk, located in another building. The kids waited on a bench and as Christine and Kevin waited, a man stepped in line behind them. They turned to acknowledge his presence and realized it was Larry. Another coincidence, they had reserved vehicles from the same company. They were called up by the next agent and gave their reservation number. As he processed their order, he gave them unexpected and pleasant news. They'd been upgraded to a seven-passenger SUV at no extra charge and Christine was thrilled. They signed the paperwork and got directions to pick up the vehicle. Leaving the counter, they motioned for the kids to join them, as Larry stepped up to the same agent. They overheard that he'd also been upgraded to the same type of vehicle. But apparently, that was not a good thing for him. Christine didn't know why, and she never asked. Larry stood at the counter arguing loudly, making the agent visibly uncomfortable. Larry called over to Christine and asked what vehicle they got. As she'd overheard his conversation, she said, "The same one they want to give you and it's perfect for us." They left in search of their vehicle choosing not to wait for Patricia and Larry. There was no way to know how long it would take for their rental issue to be resolved.

It was a two-hour drive to their destination, so they stopped in a town along the way to eat lunch, stock up at the liquor store, and get the groceries they would need for the week. It wasn't until they were already on the road again, that she finally heard from Patricia asking what they were doing for lunch. She told her they'd already eaten and weren't far from the hotel.

Their suite at the hotel, complete with kitchen and living room, turned out to be perfect for the week. Christine and Jessica, Todd's wife, had spent hours on the phone discussing meal options. With Christine's family of four and Todd's family of five, it would be much more affordable to prepare meals in their suites than go out every time. They planned daily breakfasts and dinners, knowing that some days the kids would be on the hill for lunch and would eat at the chalet. They were so glad they did. It proved to be a great bonding time too.

When the bride and groom-to-be arrived, their room was not as they had expected. It became such an issue that there was talk of changing hotels, never staying there again, writing bad reviews, etc. Christine remembered it being so taxing, she simply wanted to stay away from it all. She learned about the same time that Larry and Patricia had upgraded their room to a larger suite in case Samantha needed help with her young kids, only three and a year and a half at the time. When she heard that, Christine had looked Larry square in the eye and told him not to let Samantha take advantage of them. He assured her he would not.

Todd turned 40 a few weeks earlier but was out of town working at the time, so he hadn't enjoyed much of a celebration. That Sunday, it would be Todd's oldest daughter, Brittany's, birthday so Christine had called Jessica asking if they could host a surprise birthday party for both Todd and Brittany given her birthday was so close. They planned it for March 17th to disguise it as a St. Patrick's Day party. Christine had pre-ordered a cake from the local grocery store, complete with the birthday names written in icing. She made sure Samantha and Patricia were also aware of the surprise party plans. One thing led to another and they all decided to go in on a birthday present together. Samantha offered to order it on her end and have it in time to bring for the trip. Then Samantha slipped in that since HER daughter, Chelsea's birthday was the following month, could they add her name to the cake, too? Christine rolled her eyes. She told me she didn't often hear from Samantha unless she was asking for something. She told Samantha the cake had already been ordered and her response was, "Can't you change it?" Christine told me how difficult it was for her to keep her mouth shut. She felt badly that she didn't have a relationship with her sister's kids, and she tried to keep in mind that her relationship with their mother shouldn't have any bearing on her interaction with them, but unfortunately it did.

I could see that simply the act of retelling these stories was draining for Christine. And we hadn't even gotten to the wedding day yet. I can't imagine what it must have been like to be living that truth in real life. She agreed it was enough for one day and booked her next appointment.

CHAPTER 8

Sarah: A Secret Brother

A long-time client of mine, Sarah typically reaches out when she needs assistance reflecting on and dissecting her reactions to family-related circumstances. On this occasion, some recent interactions had been weighing heavily on her and was the reason I found her in my office that *year*.

Sarah had shared many corners of her life in past conversations, yet this one had, until that day, surprisingly remained undisclosed. She told me that her life had changed for the better on December 23rd, 14 years earlier. It was the Sunday before Christmas, the year her first child had been born. It had the shaping of being an exciting time in their lives, their son's first Christmas. Little did she know.

It was a Sunday, and Sarah's dad called, just like he did every week. She had been up in her son's room changing his diaper and had her in-laws visiting. Sarah was making a huge turkey dinner to celebrate Christmas a few days early, as she, her husband, and her son were leaving to visit her dad for the holidays.

Sarah's parents had been divorced for years, and her relationship with her dad had remained strong, even though she hadn't lived with him since she was very young. Her relationship with her mother, who had raised her, was a story for another day.

Sarah's husband had heard the phone ring and came to see who it was. As she handed their son off to him, her dad asked if she had a moment. It was an unusual request from him, and Sarah remembers hesitating before replying, "Sure." The words her dad spoke next changed her life forever.

He told her that two years before she'd been born, he and her mother had a baby boy they had given up for adoption. He had received a letter from him, their first contact, and he'd wanted Sarah to know.

As he spoke, Sarah remembers being cognizant of sitting in the nursery rocking chair, but not knowing how she got there. She recalls rocking slowly back and forth in shocked silence. She heard her dad ask if she was still there, and in a voice that was barely a whisper, Sarah told him to continue.

Her dad explained that her grandparents on her mother's side had said they could only keep the baby if they were married. Unfortunately, Sarah's mother, who had not yet turned eighteen, couldn't legally sign their marriage certificate. Since it was obvious that her parents wouldn't sign it on her behalf, they were forced to give the baby up for adoption.

She learned his name was David and that he lived in Springfield, 1250 miles away from Sarah.

Since they would be visiting her dad in a few days, he suggested they read the letter and reply together. Sarah remembers nodding into the phone, mumbling an incoherent version of good-bye, and hanging up.

She then remembered making her way downstairs in a daze and asking her husband for help upstairs, assuring him it would only take a minute. When she broke the news to him, they stood in stunned silence for a moment, before deciding that it would be best to postpone their conversation. They joined her in-laws back downstairs, but Sarah said she spent the rest of the day in a complete fog feeling like she needed to pinch herself to come back to reality.

A few days later, after having arrived at her dad's, he showed Sarah the letter.

She smiled at me, recalling what a great introduction it had been, with David giving them topline updates about his life and where he was living.

One of the things that he had come right out and announced in the letter was that he was gay and that he shared his life with his partner, Curtis. They had been together for almost eight years and married for five at that point. Sarah wondered how they'd feel about being uncles.

After talking excitedly about all the news they'd learned about David, Sarah and her dad began composing their responses separately. Sarah still remembers how she started hers. It read, "All my life, I have said that I'm an only child, with a half-brother and half-sister. Now I find out I have a full-blooded birth brother. Wow, I'm still trying to digest that."

Sarah went on to tell him a bit about her life, sharing that she was married and that she and her husband had welcomed a son earlier that year. After Sarah and her dad combined the details they agreed were appropriate as their first response back to David, they hit send. And then, they waited. And waited. A few weeks went by before the email was discovered in David's spam folder, and the relief she experienced upon hearing back from him was overwhelming.

Sarah had included her email address should he choose to respond to her directly, which he did. As she read the first few lines of his reply, her heart sank, and she almost wished that she'd never written to him in the first place. In his email to her, David had explained that he and Sarah's mom, his biological mother as well, had already been in contact through postal mail for over a year and a half before David had contacted their father. Their letters had been routed via the adoption agency, with no direct contact or knowledge of each other's addresses. In one letter, Sarah's mother had even told him that she was remarried with three other children.

As she continued taking in every word of David's email, he went on to explain that he would never have made contact, had he known that his biological parents had stayed together AND had another child that they'd kept. Sarah tried to put herself in David's shoes, but couldn't imagine the pain he must have felt, knowing he'd been given up for adoption but that his parents had kept his younger sister. Sarah felt sick to her stomach. She divulged that, to this day, she still feels extreme sadness at being the one to reveal that information to him.

Sarah moved on to happier memories and laughed as she remembered that David had called her Barbara Walters one day, in response to her seemingly endless line of questioning. This new bond had filled Sarah's life with joy and happiness, and they spent the first few months of the new year getting to know each other, through emails and phone calls.

A few months into their newly found sibling relationship, Sarah's unspoken wishes came true during a phone call with David. He said that he and Curtis had been talking and decided that it was finally time to come and meet her. "What do you think about that?" David had asked. Sarah wasn't able to contain her excitement. She thought it was awesome. She was honored that they were the first ones David wanted to meet and so soon in the grand scheme of things! It was in this spirit of excitement that plans were made. David and Curtis would fly into town to arrive at Sarah's house near the end of April.

As plans for their visit were being confirmed, Sarah realized that she and her mother had not yet discussed David or the fact that she even knew about him. David and Sarah decided it would be best to let her know before they met in person. Since their mother had kept this secret for over thirty-two years, Sarah was certain that she probably wasn't the best person to make the announcement. And so, David would write their mother a letter, letting her know that he'd made contact with his sister and that he and Curtis were scheduled to visit Sarah and her family. Before sending the letter, David sent Sarah a copy to review, confirming the day it was scheduled to arrive.

The day of delivery came, and went. Sarah waited. She was beginning to feel a pattern. A few more days went by, and she continued to wait. Finally, on a Tuesday evening, her phone rang. It was her mother. Sarah answered, and her mother, foregoing any traditional greeting, started the conversation with, "So, you know." It was more of a statement than a question.

Sarah acknowledged that she did, and her mother asked if she had any questions. She did not. Her only question had already been answered by her father, which was why she hadn't been told sooner. He had explained that no one knew if David was aware he'd been adopted, and everyone thought if she knew, that she would go looking for him. Sarah denied that she would have done any such thing, but everyone laughed at her hilarity. They were right, that was the first thing she would have done.

She then attempted to explain her outlook to her mother. The way she viewed it was there was nothing she could have done to change any part of the circumstances. She hadn't been born when it happened and had no part in the decision. The only thing she could do, and the only responsibility she felt she had moving forward, was to build a relationship with him. She informed her mother that was her plan.

To this day, Sarah believes her mother was surprised and even disappointed by her response, that she expected her to be angry, or to have more questions. But Sarah was content with the information she'd already received and felt it was all she needed to know.

Leading up to David and Curtis' visit, her mother had asked specifics about when they were arriving, how long they were staying, etc. A few days before their arrival, Sarah's mother unexpectedly announced she would be coming to visit at the same time. When David and Curtis showed up a week later, it was the first time they were all in the same room together.

Regardless of the uninvited guest, the first visit for Sarah and David was marvelous. It proved to be the beginning of a very close relationship. Even now, she and her brother talk regularly. He's great at reaching out to touch base, and when he's in town on business, he extends his trips to spend time with Sarah and her family. Not only that but when Curtis is in town alone on business, he does the same. It couldn't have turned out any better.

Shortly after their introduction, Sarah's family grew once again, to include a daughter. It was around this time that David shared that, because they didn't have any heirs of their own, he and Curtis had changed the beneficiaries of their wills to Sarah's kids. She was beyond touched.

When Sarah's half-brother got married a few years later, David and Curtis were invited and chose to attend, even though they'd never met the bride or groom. That was one of the first times it became common knowledge, to anyone outside of their immediate family, that David even existed. Although it was commonplace for Sarah to talk about her brothers or the Guncles as they love to be called, it was something new for everyone else.

After the wedding, it became apparent that Sarah's stepfather did not seem impressed with the situation. Sarah wondered if it was because he'd just had a second child from his wife's ex, dumped in his lap after having raised Sarah, or if he simply wasn't comfortable with David being gay? All she knew is that, even now, he doesn't come to visit when David is in town, and whenever they're around each other, there is a palpable awkwardness.

Sarah continued to share some of the puzzling circumstances she'd found herself in as her family adapted to the addition of David in their lives.

One weekend she was visiting her mother and stepfather on her own, about four years after learning about David. One of her mother's closest cousins was also visiting, and the three of them were up late that night, enjoying some adult beverages when Sarah mentioned David in passing. Her mother's cousin asked who David was, and as Sarah looked at her mother with a questioning expression, her mother simply nodded, seemingly permitting Sarah to continue. So Sarah continued, briefly explaining who he was, before going on with her story. Not much more was said about it that night.

Later that week, after Sarah had returned home, her mother called. Without saying hello, she blasted Sarah for outing her about David. Sarah, who was understandably shocked by her mother's ranting, said after four years there's no way she could know who her mother had and hadn't told. Her mother didn't pause to consider Sarah's perspective. This was a cousin who she had been close to for 50 years. She had kept this secret from her all this time and now she would wonder what else she'd lied about through the years. Swallowing her own emotions, Sarah told her mother she understood, but she could not be held responsible for the fact that she had chosen not to tell her cousin. Well, Sarah told me, apparently, she could.

Despite these little hiccups and their physical distance from each other, Sarah's relationship with her big brother continued to strengthen. They learned to trust one another as confidants and friends and were proud to be siblings.

Sarah confided in me that it comforts her to have found that bond with him, someone who she knows won't judge her (much), or tell her secrets. Sarah expressed how blessed she feels to have both David and Curtis in her life.

This is where Sarah needed to bounce some of her reflections off of me. She had already made the decision that her brother would be a big part of her life. The question that lingered was how present her mother would be.

Looking back, she feels that when her mother got pregnant with David, it was the beginning of the end of her mother's happiness. Sarah was clear that she was not blaming this on David, obviously, and that she wishes things could have been different for her mother. But they weren't. From the tender age of sixteen, her mother was forced to hide her secret and carry that lie for more than 30 years. What a sad life to live. But many do.

That unhappiness has permeated Sarah's mom's life. Her second and current marriage, in Sarah's eyes, has proven to be unbearable and toxic. Being around them is taxing, and she admitted that their visits have a 24-hour limit; if they're together for longer, tension builds. Even her kids are reluctant to spend more than a dinner with them. It's gotten to a point where Sarah's mom has noticed the tension and has told Sarah that she and her husband feel that they are a burden she and her family are simply tolerating.

Sarah could not disagree with her mother's observation. She also could not understand why someone would choose a life filled with so much unhappiness and discontent.

Sarah was unsure of where to go from here. While excited at the prospect of continuing to forge a strong bond with her brother, she wondered if she should put her feelings aside. Should she attempt to include her mother and embrace a relationship amongst the three of them? At this, I asked her point-blank, "Why do you feel you need to spend time with someone who drains your energy?" I could see Sarah thinking about my question before she finally responded, "Well, technically we're family and families are supposed to spend time together." She was less sure of how to answer my next question when I asked, "Says who?"

Coming into our conversation, in Sarah's mind, her options were blurry. After careful contemplation and review of the factors that were most important and healthy to her, her decision seemed so much lighter.

CHAPTER 9

Elizabeth (Part 1): Not for Lack of Trying

It was after my conversation that *year* with Elizabeth that I truly wished there was a magic pill that when swallowed, would increase a person's level of self-awareness. That thought was not directed towards Elizabeth herself, but at the woman her father had married after her parents' divorce.

Her dad, Frank, had remarried almost 25 years ago. At that point, Elizabeth's parents had already been divorced for 15 years. Frank's new wife, Gail, already had two daughters, Joy and Shawna, who at the time of the wedding were nine and seven years old. Frank had been in their lives from their earliest childhood memories. Gail's first husband was killed in a tragic car accident. But there was alcohol involved and after his death, she attempted, albeit unsuccessfully, to sue a handful of their friends who had let him drink too much that night.

Not long after her first husband's death, Gail's father, whom she was also very close to, died suddenly of a heart attack. Within six short months, she lost the two men that meant the most to her, a difficult time for even the strongest of women to navigate. With a toddler and an infant, there were going to be tough times ahead for her.

Elizabeth and I agreed that these unfathomable events happening so close in sequence would undoubtedly take its toll on anyone. The support you would need to get through something like that would be immeasurable. And, it could have a long-lasting impact if it wasn't dealt with fully or properly and in a timely manner.

Based on Elizabeth's recount, that is what I perceive had happened. Gail never fully dealt with her grief and, in Elizabeth's eyes, she lived a very unhappy life as a result. As Elizabeth lived about three hundred and fifty miles away, she wasn't exposed to the issues regularly, but it seemed evident that whenever they were together, Gail's unhappiness persisted.

Elizabeth started at the beginning when she first became aware that Gail would become a mainstay in her life. One weekend, when Elizabeth was still in high school, she'd gone to visit her dad. He drove her to an unfamiliar house and told her it was his friend's younger sister's place, that her husband had recently died, and that she felt more comfortable having a man around the house. Elizabeth didn't remember if, at that time, he was staying in a spare room or sleeping on the couch. Nonetheless it was convenient for him as well because he had been looking for a new place to live. At least that's what he had told her. Elizabeth doesn't remember much of that visit other than meeting Gail and her young daughters for the first time.

A few months later when Elizabeth returned to visit her dad, they again drove to Gail's house straight from the train station. The daughters were about four and two years old by then. Elizabeth was told to put her bag in the spare room and had commented about where her dad would sleep that night. The four-year-old piped up, "Oh, he sleeps in my mommy's bed." And that was how Elizabeth had come to know that her dad and Gail were a couple.

Looking back, Elizabeth had always known that Gail had insecurities. Elizabeth was forbidden from mentioning the names of any women Frank had previously dated, anytime Gail was present. Gail was very sensitive and not warm towards Elizabeth at all in the beginning. As young as she was, Elizabeth had already started to recognize the signs of someone projecting their issues onto her. She sensed Gail perceived her as a threat who might someday take her dad away. At the time, she didn't pay it much regard.

When Elizabeth was in her first year of university, Frank called to tell her that he and Gail were getting married. He bought plane tickets for Elizabeth and her then-boyfriend to attend the wedding. She recalled playing the role of a pseudo-bridesmaid of sorts. She walked up the aisle with Gail's two daughters, hand in hand, and sat near the front during the ceremony. Her dad had officially adopted the girls the day before the wedding. It was nice to see him happy. The night of his wedding, when Elizabeth was dancing with him, she asked him if he was happy and he told her he was. She told him that's all that mattered to her.

After the wedding, Elizabeth thought Gail's insecurities might settle down, satisfied that they were now married. It would be harder for Elizabeth to split them up, something Gail always seemed afraid she would attempt to do. To this day, Elizabeth believes, deep down Gail still has those insecurities.

Not surprisingly, Elizabeth and Gail had a stilted relationship. To Elizabeth it seemed like Gail looked for fault at every turn. She reprimanded her for the way she treated her daughters. According to Gail, one was very sensitive and warranted a delicate touch when interacting with her. The other was a little more rough and tumble and could manage a tougher approach. While being required to decipher which mood they were in, Elizabeth also had to remember to treat them differently but also according to their frame of mind on any given day. The hoops she was forced to jump through simply to keep Gail happy were never-ending. On one particular visit, Frank and Gail decided to go out, announcing that Elizabeth would babysit the girls. She was also ordered to cut the grass while they were gone and was puzzled to have been given these duties. She didn't live there. They weren't providing for her or paying any of her bills. Elizabeth decided to cut the grass anyway leaving the girls, 11 and 9, and old enough at the time, with instructions to play inside until she was done. While she was mowing the front, Frank and Gail pulled up at the back of the house and went inside, unbeknownst to her. Gail came screaming out the front door, yelling that the girls were gone. Elizabeth stopped the lawnmower and asked her to repeat what she'd said because she hadn't heard her over the noise. By then, her dad also appeared as Gail continued screaming at her, "Where are the girls? We left you in charge. Where are they?" Elizabeth told her she'd left them instructions to stay inside while she cut the grass and that was the last she saw them. Frank and Gail ran off to look for the girls, who they found a few minutes later playing at the next-door neighbors'.

Once they were deemed safe and unharmed, Frank and Gail made their way back to where Elizabeth had continued cutting the grass. Gail wanted to know why she hadn't been watching the girls while they were gone. Elizabeth asked her how she expected her to watch her girls AND mow their lawn at the same time. And questioned why Gail wasn't mad at the girls for not listening to instructions and leaving the house without telling her. Gail looked at Frank, pointed at Elizabeth, and said, "FIX HER!" To that, Elizabeth had replied, "I'm not a machine. You can't just fix me." and she left.

Their awkward relationship, coupled with the distance that separated them in Elizabeth's adult life, provided for limited interactions between Elizabeth, her dad, and his family. That pattern continued as Elizabeth met and married her husband, Rick, and prior to them having kids; she was completely fine with that. They were each busy living their own lives.

A few months after Elizabeth announced she was pregnant with their first child, she received a call from Gail, who had been wondering what role she would play in the baby's life. Elizabeth asked her directly what role she wanted to play. Gail said she wanted to be one of the grandmothers. Elizabeth hadn't expected anything different. And so it was, they became Grandma Gail and Grandpa Frank.

Elizabeth's son, Christopher, was the first grandchild on that side and fell in line as a favorite with Frank and Gail. In their eyes, he could do no wrong. Elizabeth remembered a time when Christopher was five or so. He was using the couches in their basement as a jungle gym, crawling up on the back of them and jumping down. Elizabeth had asked him to stop for two reasons. He shouldn't have been using the furniture like a gymnasium and secondly, she didn't want him to get hurt. He chose not to listen and within minutes, had fallen off the couch and smacked his head on the coffee table.

Elizabeth picked him up and held him while he cried and checked his head to make sure there was no blood. Once he stopped crying, she told him that the reason she'd asked him to stop playing on the couches was so he wouldn't get hurt. He understood why and acknowledged that if he'd stopped when she'd asked, he wouldn't have suffered the consequences.

Just as Elizabeth got up to do something else, Gail scooped Christopher up in her arms and sat on the couch with him. Elizabeth was still within earshot and able to hear her lean into Christopher's ear to whisper that he didn't do anything wrong and he shouldn't have gotten into trouble. Elizabeth, not wanting to create a scene, said nothing. Undermining her authority as a parent had become a popular practice of Gail's.

While Christopher remained a favorite, Elizabeth felt that her younger daughter, Tiffany, didn't really exist in Gail's eyes. She focused her love and attention on Christopher and seemed to often dismiss Tiffany. She had also noticed that whenever Gail and Frank came to visit, Gail would plunk herself down on the couch in their living room with a magazine and hardly move the entire weekend. Elizabeth recounted a story that still stings her to retell to this day. While prepping a large dinner for the weekend's celebrations, Elizabeth's younger sister had called. She was making a turkey for the first time and had a ton of questions for Elizabeth. After providing copious instructions, Elizabeth hung up the phone with a smile on her face. Gail had overheard the whole conversation and didn't waste any time asking why her sister was calling Elizabeth for directions. Although she didn't say it outright, the impression she gave was that Elizabeth was the last person who should be helping someone else in the kitchen. To make up for his wife's lack of filter, Frank exclaimed wildly at dinner how delicious the food was after every single bite. It pained Elizabeth that Gail had put her dad in that position. In hindsight, Elizabeth suspected that Gail was dragged along for visits against her will. It wasn't long after that when Frank started coming on his own, which was a relief for everyone.

Fast forward a few years to a time when Gail's younger daughter, Shawna, was about to get married. Gail was looking for a Mother-of-the-Bride dress and since they were planning to be at Elizabeth's for Easter, she had asked if she knew of any fancy dress stores. Elizabeth told her she absolutely did and selected a few stores they could visit. She had even mapped out the best route to take to be able to hit them all in one day. She had originally planned to serve dinner on the day Gail wanted to go shopping, so Elizabeth changed the day and then ensured everyone else who was invited for dinner could change their plans as well.

The day dawned bright and sunny, as Elizabeth described it, perfect for a day of dress shopping. But Gail decided that she wanted to take the kids to the park and visit their favorite bakery first. So, they all piled into Elizabeth's minivan, drove to the park and then the bakery, which took hours, eating away at the dress shopping time. By the time they got home, it was mid-afternoon. As they were pulling up to the house, Elizabeth asked if they were all set to go dress shopping. Gail said, "Yes, the four of us are, Frank, Shawna, Joe (husband-to-be), and me." Elizabeth sat in stunned silence. They had been planning to go shopping together for the past two months. She hadn't gotten the memo that she was no longer invited. Elizabeth parked the van, got the kids and without saying a word, went into the house. Her husband, Rick, looked concerned and questioned if they would still have enough time to go dress shopping. Elizabeth told him it didn't matter and that apparently, she wasn't going. Rick was equally shocked knowing they had been planning it for months.

Frank must have sensed Elizabeth's mood change. He had come into the house under the pretense of saying goodbye, but Elizabeth believes he also wanted to see if she was okay. She let loose. She told him she was tired of Gail hating her and in turn, hating Tiffany. She believed it was because she was so much like her mother and a constant reminder to Gail of Frank's previous marriage. And Tiffany was so much like Elizabeth, she didn't like her for the same reasons. Frank assured her that wasn't the case, that she was just insecure about how she looked and only wanted family to come dress shopping with her. Elizabeth said she should have told her that from the beginning instead of creating this mess. Her dad left at that point, they went dress shopping and the rest of their visit was notably tense.

That summer, Elizabeth recounted driving the eight hours to be in attendance at the wedding. They'd spent a long day in the vehicle with their young kids and had arrived shortly after dinner time. Gail proceeded to tell them she was too tired to feed them and if they wanted to eat, there was food in the fridge. Joy, the older daughter, said, "Mom, they just drove hours to be here. You have to feed them." Joy helped them get the kids fed before they left for their hotel room, as more important guests had been invited to stay at the house.

One fall, Frank and Gail visited for Thanksgiving along with Rick's parents and brother. They realized it had been ten or eleven years since they'd all been in the same room together, at Elizabeth and Rick's wedding. Everyone agreed it would be a great idea to take a photo with all of them together again, this time including the kids. Rick got the camera set up in front of the spot on the stairs where they took so many group shots in their house. They all gathered together, making sure to leave room for Rick after he set the timer on the camera. That's when Elizabeth saw Gail sitting on the couch with her magazine. She invited her to get in the picture to which Gail replied, "I don't do pictures." Others tried to persuade her to join. Gail just sat there and didn't move. She didn't even offer to take the picture having chosen not to be in it. Elizabeth was speechless. After they got a few poses captured, Elizabeth grabbed a beer and went out on her front step and drank the whole thing down. (I'll interject that Elizabeth did not have a drinking problem or rely often on alcohol to drown her sorrows.) She took a deep breath and came back in to finish cooking their turkey dinner. That was the last time they were all in the same room together as Rick's mom passed away suddenly not long afterward. So sad.

It wasn't as though Elizabeth didn't try to have a better relationship with Gail. She told me of one particular Christmas when Shawna and her husband, Joe, were going to be home. Elizabeth made secret arrangements with them to drive up a few days after Christmas to surprise Frank and Gail. Gail's birthday falls between Christmas and New Years and was the day they planned to arrive. Elizabeth had stopped to get a huge bouquet of roses for Gail's birthday and upon arrival at the house,

Elizabeth rang the doorbell, pretending to be a flower delivery. She hid behind the bouquet and it wasn't until Gail took it out of her hands and then looked directly at her, that it clicked. That's when the rest of Elizabeth's family came around the corner and surprised her.

The "big kicker that has yet to be resolved" as Elizabeth called it, happened on Christmas night when the kids were 10 and 8. Gail had learned that for the first time, neither of her girls were coming home for Christmas. Elizabeth and her family typically vacation somewhere hot over Christmas, but that year they had a big trip booked for March, so they'd be staying local. Frank hinted that maybe they could come for a visit.

Elizabeth took that opportunity to explain to me what had been decided when her kids were firstborn. She and Rick were firm that for the kids' sake, they would spend Christmas Eve and Christmas morning at their own home to welcome Santa. Anyone who wanted could visit Christmas Eve and if there were enough beds, they could stay over and wake up Christmas morning with them. They had decided this would be the least disruptive and most enjoyable way for their kids to enjoy Christmas while they were young. It also prevented the need to decline family invitations over another, which had previously resulted in hurt feelings.

That year, Elizabeth and Rick had discussed visiting Frank and Gail on the 27th or 28th for just a few days. Frank talked to Gail about them potentially coming up when Gail had asked if they could arrive before Christmas so they could see the kids open their presents Christmas morning. Elizabeth and Rick's immediate reaction was - NO WAY. They only slept in their own beds Christmas Eve and nothing was going to change that. In hindsight,

Elizabeth said they should have listened. They had done it that way for the kids, who were now older, old enough to be part of the discussion and decision. The kids decided they might enjoy spending the entire time with their grandparents. They called Grandpa Frank and told him they'd be up on the night of the 23rd, a Friday, and would be able to stay until the following Wednesday. They'd wake up with Grandma on her birthday and then get on the road.

Elizabeth and I realized at that point how quickly our time had flown. She had another appointment to get to and promised we'd pick up where we left off the following week. I was really interested to find out how this Christmas visit turned out, hoping it was the reset with Gail that she so desperately needed.

CHAPTER 10

Emily: UPAL

Emily and I had known each other for a while, so parts of this story were scattered across our many meetings. I knew she was profoundly fond of her relationship with UPAL so I was puzzled when she came to me with doubts that *year*.

UPAL is her acronym for Uncle Pete and Aunt Linda, and it couldn't have been more appropriate. Their bond had been inked years prior and, in my opinion, should never have been questioned. She had shared with me how they'd become a staple in her life, along with additional stories as they came to mind. It took some concentration to follow along, but the end result was clear.

Emily's story picked up as she headed to university hundreds of miles away from home. The realization started to sink in that she'd only have a few friends and family close by. With her footing her own bill for school, she'd lucked out in terms of a place to live. She was moving into an apartment that was geared to income just two blocks from the school. The one Emily was placed in had five bedrooms, two bathrooms, and a common kitchen and living area. You didn't get to choose who you lived with, but at seventy-five dollars a month, including utilities, the price was right. With friends paying over fifteen times that amount to live across the street, Emily felt very fortunate. The only extras she would have to pay for were food and her phone – the old-fashioned kind with a spiral cord that plugged into the wall. Emily ended up living in that apartment building for exactly four years, two in the five-bedroom, then a two-bedroom two floors up for the final two. In the smaller unit, Emily's rent did increase to, as she put it, "a whopping ninety-six dollars a month". If she hadn't found such an affordable place to live, Emily isn't sure that she would have made it through university, financially speaking.

Emily spent her first year at university getting her feet under her. She picked up part-time work waitressing at an event hall and was an on-call nanny for a family with three kids. Between school and work, she stayed busy.

On the surface, while Emily's plate seemed pretty full, she was finding it very lonely. She spent most holidays at her friend Jillian's, which helped. Emily had met Jillian a few years earlier, and a fast friendship had formed, growing out of their mutual love of a local sports team. Before long, they'd found themselves watching games together as often as they could. As they got to know each other, Emily learned that Jillian's parents were divorced. When she wasn't at school, Jillian lived with her mom and sister. They always welcomed Emily whenever she arrived, and she enjoyed visiting them. It had been nice to have somewhere to go that felt like home.

But Jillian was at school an hour away, and her house was another hour past that. It wasn't easy for Emily to get there, especially without a car.

Because she was feeling so lonely, Emily decided to reach out to her Uncle Pete and Aunt Linda, her stepfather's brother and his wife. They lived just over half an hour away, but with traffic or transit, travel times could easily exceed an hour. She recalled how readily they had opened their arms to Emily from the first time they'd met, and she hoped they might be just the antidote she needed. It turned out that Uncle Pete worked in the city, not too far from Emily's apartment. If she gave him enough notice, he'd come by to pick her up on any given Friday afternoon so Emily could spend the weekend with them. On Sunday night, they'd take her to the station to catch a bus back into the city. Some nights, they even took her all the way to the subway. Emily remembers thinking that Uncle Pete and Aunt Linda's house was what home was supposed to feel like. They had two young children who felt more like her little brother and sister than her cousins. Emily quickly developed an incredibly warm, close relationship with the whole family. Despite all the good that Uncle Pete and Aunt Linda brought into her life, their presence began to raise questions for Emily. The juxtaposition between her home life growing up and the feeling she experienced simply walking through their doors, was eye-opening. There were days when she'd spend hours picking apart her own memories, trying to figure out where she'd gone awry as a kid, or what she'd done wrong all her life. Why hadn't she known what a real home filled with love felt like until now?

That isn't to say they didn't have their problems, as any family does. Uncle Pete and Aunt Linda still dealt with real-life issues, but they made sure that Emily was never a part of it. Their love for her was unconditional, and she knew it. This wasn't something Emily had experienced with her own family, so it was an entirely new feeling for her. It was hard to believe that they weren't even a blood relation since their connection to Emily stemmed only through her stepfather, Carl. They enjoyed laughing at the irony of it, and believe theirs is a connection even deeper than blood. They are certain they were connected in a past life, and have once again come together to live a life intertwined. She giggled as she admitted this to me, but it was hard to overlook the sincerity in her eyes.

About ten years prior to our conversation that day, Emily had an incredibly emotional epiphany. She'd been doing some soul searching, trying to figure out WHY her stepfather was a part of her life. To what purpose had Carl been put in her path? For as long as I've known Emily, she has always been a firm believer that everyone who crosses your path does so for a very specific reason. Until that point, she'd been unable to find any explanation for why she'd had to endure Carl's presence in her life. It had then dawned on her, and when it did, she cried as if she'd been saving up tears her entire life. Without Carl, there would be no UPAL. Without them, she would never have known about the void that had existed in her life. Emily acknowledged that if they were taken from her for any reason, the chasm created by their absence could never again be bridged; the thought always takes her breath away. They have always been there for her. They were the only constant in her life for years. They don't judge her or make her feel like she's made wrong or bad choices. They don't tell her how to raise her kids. They simply love her and honor her, and that is exactly what they get from Emily in return.

When there is news to share, most of Emily's friends and relatives pick up the phone to call their parents. For Emily, UPAL is always her first call. If a week goes by where she hasn't had at least an hour to catch up with Aunt Linda over the phone, a part of her feels missing. Their calls are marked by so much hilarity, Emily typically hangs up with sore abs from all the laughing. She frequently has to ask Aunt Linda if she's ok, as when she is laughing so hard, she doesn't make any noise. During those times, Emily waits for her to catch her breath, ensures everything is alright and then they laugh some more. UPAL knew that Emily was getting married, and having babies, before her own parents did. After years of its non-existence in her life, she finally understood what a healthy relationship looked like, and that what she feels when she is with UPAL – the way they make her feel – has become her normal. And, that normal is what she tries to model in her own relationships.

Instead of finding the positive in their relationship, Emily's family has plenty of questions about why things are so good with them. They ask Emily, "What do they have that we don't?" Why do you love them so much?" It's hard for Emily to explain to her parents and siblings, but what she has with UPAL is nothing more than a healthy, loving relationship. For Emily, the biggest comfort in their relationship is the lack of judgment. It's pretty simple, and yet it means everything to her. She will never give it up. What continues to puzzle Emily about her family's curiosity is that they've seen other unique family relationships develop without issue. When Carl's mom was still alive, Emily's brother was clearly her favorite grandchild. Another aunt and uncle have a very special bond with her sister. Why does her family seem to think that Emily's relationship with UPAL requires a different lens?

While strange, it's not her family's curiosity about her relationship with UPAL that bothers Emily the most. The problem is that, for years, her family has made her feel like the relationship somehow makes her a bad person.

They've never accepted it, for reasons Emily will probably never understand. Because of this, she often feels like her family is silently punishing her for the bond she shares with her aunt and uncle. Why should she be punished? Why is her happiness such a problem for her family? Emily has to work to quiet these questions when they arise, and does so by reminding herself of what's important: that UPAL knows exactly how deep Emily's love for them is. No question. And isn't that how it should be? What is more important in life than finding people to love unconditionally and letting them know how much they mean to you, as often as you can?

Emily feels pretty sure her relationship with UPAL is the only thing that kept her going through some of the darkest times in her life. Her early twenties were tough and, while suicide is an awful thought, she admitted it ran through her mind, more than once. When it did, Emily's thoughts would immediately go to, "Where do I turn, to find a port in this storm?" Her answer was always, UPAL. For Emily, they were a soft place to fall, and somewhere she could always turn. Uncle Pete helped her move more times than she can remember, let alone count. In those days, Emily always made sure to thank him – she knows she did, because her gratitude was all she had to offer in return; her gratitude, and her love. They made her feel like that was enough.

At one point during university, Emily attempted to repair her relationship with Carl and her mother, Brenda. Her parents had recently relocated to a new town for Carl's job and had invited Emily to visit. As they were discussing arrangements, they mentioned that the bus would drop Emily off on the main road, at the corner of the long road her parents lived on. While she was no stranger to bus travel, Emily had gotten so accustomed to Uncle Pete's offers to meet her half-way that this was jarring for her. She didn't know what she had expected, but it wasn't this. She didn't even know where she was going, let alone dragging a suitcase behind her! Emily had hoped they might at least offer to pick her up for her first trip, but no such offer materialized.

Another invite came after Carl and Brenda moved to another house in town. Emily already had plans to celebrate a friend's birthday that weekend so she initially declined the invitation. Brenda persisted, offering Emily the use of her car on Saturday night. Emily could keep her plans and return the car to Brenda and Carl's house on Sunday. Even though the offer made the decision easier for Emily, she's not sure why she agreed. She spent time with them on the Saturday until it was time to leave for the birthday celebrations, a three-hour drive away. That Sunday, when she returned with Brenda's car, she learned her mom had expected her to be up at dawn to drive back. The hostility that radiated from Brenda upon her return was so toxic, Emily is rattled by the memory to this day. She assessed the situation and made an immediate exit. Walking from the middle of town to the highway, Emily hitched a ride with a nice woman who happily drove her all the way back to the city. At the time, Emily had realized that she had to choose between her happiness and their misery. She never visited that house again.

Experiences like that helped Emily decide the type of person she wanted to be. She vowed that any time she had the opportunity to welcome a visitor to her home, she would do whatever she could to make sure they were comfortable and happy. If that meant driving to pick someone up so they could visit, she would do it. If it meant grabbing someone from the airport after their flight, that's where she'd be. If something was in her power to do for one of her guests, then she would do it willingly. She knew the little things would mean a lot in the long run.

Despite the serenity with which she continued to describe her relationship with UPAL, things weren't rosy on all fronts. Carl and Brenda's strange animosity toward Emily's relationship with UPAL continued to color almost every interaction. Emily said she did her best to take it in stride, but admitted it wasn't always easy. When she graduated from university, Uncle Pete and Aunt Linda bought her a treasured full-size Royal Doulton figurine. In a strange turn of chance, Carl and Brenda gave her a miniature Royal Doulton figurine, as well as money. Emily was grateful to have received both figurines, which were proudly displayed behind the glass of her dining room hutch. During a visit, her mother noticed the figurines and asked Emily about the larger one. For a moment, Emily considered telling her a lie. It would have made for a more pleasant conversation. But she was tired of going down that road with her family, and she didn't think it would be a big issue, anyway. Emily told her that Pete and Linda gave it to her for graduation. And as Emily predicted, Brenda took the first opportunity to turn UPAL's gift into something that it wasn't; something ugly. "They always have to be better than us, don't they?" she'd lamented. The only response she could think of at the time was a question of her own. "I got both figurines on the exact same day. How would they have known?"

UPAL were the first family members to meet Emily's future husband when they started dating. Their approval of him was immediate, and it has never wavered. Which is a good thing, because, without it, Emily doubts they would have gotten married! Uncle Pete was the MC at their wedding and Aunt Linda fitted her veil.

The day before the wedding, UPAL arrived at Emily's house bright and early. Emily's fiancé and Uncle Pete left for the wedding venue early so the guys could play a round of golf. Emily and Aunt Linda planned to leave before lunch. Aunt Linda had only seen Emily's wedding dress in photos, so Emily asked if she would finally like to see it in person. Linda told her that she wasn't ready yet, but that she'd let her know when she was.

Emily continued finalizing everything for the wedding and honeymoon, and was lost in preparations when Aunt Linda told her she was ready. The wedding dress was in a spare room, hanging over the closet door. Emily began by showing her the back and the train, which were her favorite parts. It warmed her heart to see Aunt Linda wipe the tears from her eyes. When she turned it around to show Aunt Linda the front, she said it was her aunt's expression, not the dress, that caught her attention. She did not expect the look of shock that crossed her face. Puzzled, Emily turned to look at the dress and was greeted by two glaring black stains on the front and center of the otherwise-white gown. After Emily's stomach left her throat, they figured out what had happened. There was grease on the closet door's hinges, which left two oily black stains on the dress where it had rubbed up against them. Linda and Emily discussed their options, of which there weren't many. Emily called the hotel's wedding coordinator to see if she had any suggestions. Luckily, the dry cleaner the hotel used was on their way to the venue. The two women finished packing and headed out for the one-hour drive. Despite their busy agenda, Emily and Aunt Linda took the scenic route along the lakeshore, which was a great decision. It was the end of April and the magnolia trees were in full bloom along their entire route, a magical vision. Looking back, Emily said it had seemed as if that beautiful sight had been laid out just for her, leading her to her wedding day, and to the wonderful life that she and her husband would enjoy together.

The dry cleaner proved easy to find. After Emily described what the dress had come in contact with, the dry cleaner whisked her dress to the back, disappearing from sight. Approximately two minutes later, he returned with the dress and much to Emily's surprise, the black stains were gone! He then told Emily they were delivering other items to her hotel later that day and offered to steam her dress in preparation for the ceremony. Emily took the dry cleaner up on his generous offer, and her dress arrived at the hotel looking even more perfect than she'd thought possible.

As Linda and Emily had worked up an appetite, they decided to find a restaurant nearby where they could grab a bite to eat. They sat outside, enjoying their food and the beauty of the day, and doing what they do best; they laughed. They talked about the shock they both felt at seeing the stains on Emily's wedding dress, and they laughed at the absurdity of the situation. They talked about how relieved they were that it had worked out so easily, and they laughed with gratitude. They talked about how lucky they were to be enjoying the day together, and they laughed with pure joy.

The weather was gorgeous, and unseasonably warm. When Emily's wedding invitations were printed, they stated that the ceremony would be held in The Garden. While stunning, she knew that inclement weather would most likely make this impossible, and had found a beautiful room indoors that worked perfectly for them. When they arrived at the hotel, Emily and Aunt Linda were greeted by even more trees in full flower. Making their way to the garden area, two large pink magnolia trees in full bloom took their breath away. They had grown to form a canopy exactly above the spot the ceremony would take place, provided the good weather remained. The whole scene was jaw-droppingly gorgeous. Emily stood there for a minute, feeling grateful and also wondering what she'd done to deserve such good fortune. She was so thankful she'd been able to share this unforgettable time with her Aunt Linda. As the next day dawned warm and sunny, their wedding did take place in The Garden, with all their friends and family in attendance. It was a wonderful start to their marriage.

Not long after that, when Emily and her husband bought their second family home, they had company for 30 out of 52 weekends during their first year there. She stood by the decision to be a warm and welcoming host to company, to ensure her visitors felt completely at home under her roof. Because their home was close to the airport, their driveway was often filled with extra cars, left there by friends and relatives hoping to bypass outrageous parking fees at the airport. Cars, like people, were always welcome at Emily's.

When her cousin came to town by bus to buy a new-to-him car, Emily insisted on picking him up at the bus station when he arrived, at midnight, even though the bus station was forty-five minutes from her home. He was happy to make other arrangements and had planned on doing so, but she wouldn't take no for an answer. Not only did Emily pick him up at the bus station at midnight, but she also brought him back to her house and put him up overnight. In the back of her mind the whole time, she kept asking herself, what would UPAL do, how would they be trying to make me feel in this situation? They were her compass. Her cousin knew the car was "somewhere in the metro area". This narrowed the car's potential location down to a span of about one hundred miles. As it turned out, they didn't have to go far. The car was located at a dealership just three miles from Emily's house. It couldn't have been planned better.

These were times when Emily felt most acutely aligned with the universe. She would have happily covered the entire hundred-square-mile metro area to help her cousin get to his car, but that hadn't been necessary. As a firm believer in the idea that 'you get what you give', she could feel the universe looking out for her, making it easy for her to uphold the commitments she made to both her cousin and to herself.

In a synonymous way, everything Emily puts out to UPAL comes right back to her and continues to come back to her every single day. She was recently making turkey soup and started to grind pepper into the pot using her "Homemade by Uncle Pete" pepper mill. With each turn of the handle, Emily said she could feel Uncle Pete adding love to her soup. Aching to speak to him, she picked up the phone and called. When he didn't answer, Emily left a message; "Uncle Pete, I just wanted to thank you for adding so much love to our soup today. With every turn of the pepper mill, I felt your love being added. I know that when we eat it tonight for supper, we'll be filling our bellies with your love, and I just wanted to thank you for that."

When Emily spoke to Aunt Linda later that week, she asked if Uncle Pete got the message. Her aunt said yes, and it had brought him laughter and tears when he listened to it. For Emily, this is what it means to express your love in a normal and healthy way.

When Emily's daughter was born at 1:45 am, she was excited to share the news, but waited until the morning to make her phone calls, of which there were only two. In those days, cell phones weren't allowed in hospitals, so they had to sneak the calls in between nurses' visits as it was. Finally, at about 7 am, she made her first call to UPAL, of course. Then she called Carl and Brenda, asking them to tell the rest of the family about their new addition. Carl and Brenda agreed, and Emily assumed they would be eager to tell everyone about their new granddaughter.

Later that day, Pete called his and Carl's mom, Emily's grandma. They talked about how her day had been and eventually the conversation wove around to Uncle Pete asking if she was excited about the news. She asked, "What news?" Uncle Pete's first thought was that she'd forgotten. His mom had previously suffered a stroke and now lived in a nursing home. Her memory at that point was spotty, at best, so he didn't give it much thought.

It would still be a few hours before Carl would call his mom and share the news about Emily's new daughter. They had a standing call every Wednesday at 8 pm. Rather than share the news twelve hours earlier when he said he would, Carl decided to wait until their scheduled time to tell his mom that she had a new granddaughter. When his mother told him that Pete had already informed her, it sent Carl into a tailspin. He hung up the phone and immediately called his brother. Not bothering with the formality of a greeting, he told Pete through gritted teeth, "You are not the grandparents. Stop trying to be the grandparents." Emily wouldn't learn about this exchange until a week later, when Christmas rolled around.

As Emily's family grew, it had become tradition for UPAL to spend Christmas Eve with their niece. With the arrival of Emily's daughter, this holiday promised to be a truly special one, and Emily was counting down the days until their visit. Out of the blue, Aunt Linda called to tell Emily that their plans had changed. She and Uncle Pete wouldn't be able to spend Christmas Eve with them after all. Trying to hide her disappointment, Emily asked why. Aunt Linda attempted to pass the change of plans off as something innocuous – forgotten plans, visiting relatives, or some such excuse. But Emily could sense that something was off in her aunt's reply. Curious and disappointed, Emily pressed for the truth. Linda reluctantly told her about Carl's phone call to Pete. Emily couldn't believe that she had a brand new baby to contend with, and now she had to deal with Carl and Brenda's shit, on top of that. Emily immediately called her parents. She explained to Carl and Brenda that they were uninvited for Christmas, that they would not be welcome in her home and promptly hung up the phone. After all she'd put up with, this was the last straw. She was done.

It was plain for anyone to see that Emily's relationship with UPAL was far healthier than the one she shared with her own family. Yet, in considering her options, Emily also stated it was unequivocally easier to keep the peace by making her family happy. She was being forced to decide which was more important to her. As she considered the factors that were coming into play at that time in her life, she mused on all the stories she'd shared with me. In hindsight, she admitted that recounting them out loud, to another person, made our conversation seem almost unnecessary, the decision was so obvious.

CHAPTER 11

Tracy (Part 2): The Saga Continues

When we regrouped a few weeks later, Tracy had a smile on her face. She told me when she'd left the last time, her Calgon had been found both in a bathtub and a wine glass, in the same sitting. She'd had a good night's sleep the night before and was anxious to make some headway today. We dove back in.

Tracy spent her 17th birthday alone and crying in her bedroom. It was Labor Day Monday and the next day she would be starting at her new school.

That first day was as bad as she imagined it would be. The biggest shock for her had nothing to do with the students, it was the teachers. At her old school, she knew each one, including the Principal and Vice-Principals. She had expected to feel alone, not knowing any kids. Initially, the big void was not knowing any of the staff, and quickly graduated to not knowing anyone at all.

Slowly she made friends. One of her first friends was a boy who followed her home from school that first day. He wanted to know where the new girl lived. And once she learned that he lived at the end of her street, the following her home part didn't feel so strange.

Soon she was going to parties and being helped up onto a parade float when fellow students saw her sitting on the curb with her family. It didn't take long to fit in, and when she thought about it, she hadn't expected anything different. She made friends easily. She just didn't want to be forced to.

The boyfriend she'd left behind was starting his first year of university. They tried to carry on a long-distance relationship but by Thanksgiving, he decided to end things. She admitted it was an incredibly sad time for her. And, when Wendy asked what was wrong, she laughed that they had tried to keep it going as long as they had. Tracy told me she never felt more alone in her entire life.

Gradually, life became more bearable. She got a job at a department store as a cashier. It was a great way to make some extra cash and not be forced to spend more time than necessary with her family. She made some good friends there too, ones she keeps in touch with to this day.

One of the friends had the use of her family's car to go out on the weekends. At the end of one night, after they dropped off her friend's boyfriend, they realized that he left his bottle of whiskey in the car. She told Tracy if her parents found alcohol in the car, she'd never be allowed to drive it again. So, Tracy offered to take it with her and return it to him the following weekend.

Tracy hid the bottle at the back of the middle drawer of her dresser underneath some clothes. Wendy and Chuck were aware that she drank when she was out with her friends, so she had surmised that if they found the bottle, it wouldn't be a big deal. She was wrong.

A few weeks later, they said they needed to discuss something serious with her. And what they said next made Tracy laugh out loud as she told the story... "We always knew it would come to this." They had discovered the alcohol in her bedroom and proceeded to ask how long she had been an alcoholic. Tracy laughed at their accusation and explained her friend's dilemma and that she had offered to take the bottle and return it the next weekend. They accused her of making up the story.

Just before Christmas that first year in their new town, Tracy became aware of a boy at school. She asked around, wondering who he was. He was a year younger than her and his name was Chad. She kept her eye out for him and like any teenaged girl, found her heart jumping in her chest each time she saw him coming around the corner.

She remembers writing an exam that semester. They used the gymnasium so all classes could write at the same time. After they were all seated, she looked to her left and there sat Chad. Once she'd finished writing as much of the exam as she could, she used the leftover time to write him a letter. And when they were permitted to leave, she quickly handed him the note and asked him not to read it until he got home that night.

Tracy and Chad started dating shortly after Christmas her senior year. It was the beginning of a long relationship, filled with ups and downs and a lot of growth in between. They said their final goodbyes four and a half years later. Tracy isn't sure where she'd be without having had Chad in her life. And she's not sure she ever thanked him for sticking with her through everything they endured as a couple, everything she went through with her parents during their time together.

Chad would give her notecards for special occasions and sometimes for no reason at all. That's how Tracy learned that she didn't have any privacy at home. She recalled one time when Wendy was yelling at her, she ended her rant by saying, "Why don't you run crying to Chad about this, so he can give you a card to make you feel all better?"

Tracy often felt like an outsider. When they lived in their former town, they would go downhill skiing as a family. Tracy was on the ski team and raced as often as she could. After they moved, she'd grown into wearing the same size skis as Wendy. But, they only had one pair of skis that size. If they decided to go skiing as a family, Wendy would go and Tracy was left home alone. Tracy told me she didn't put on a pair of skis again for over twenty years and had hated every minute of it.

Then there were nights they would attempt to be a normal family and go out for dinner. Tracy would feel excited by the idea of a nice meal out but, dinner out with Chuck was typically an embarrassing experience. The food was never hot enough or cooked properly. Every single meal had him sending his plate back or chastising the server for not reading his mind. It was especially humiliating if someone she knew was working at the restaurant.

One of Tracy's responsibilities at home was to have the kitchen floor washed by 11 am on Saturday, once a month. One Saturday morning she was hungover from partying the night before and she missed the 11 am deadline. As punishment, Chuck didn't talk to her for an entire month. After a month had passed, Wendy asked her to apologize so they could have some peace in the house. But Tracy told her she didn't feel it was her responsibility to repair him. Wendy begged. So, she went to Chuck and said, "Mom asked me to apologize to you for not having the floor washed on time, so I'm sorry." He didn't like that and chose not to talk to her for another month. As much as she knew it exacerbated the tension between Wendy and Chuck, she told me that she loved the peace and quiet, knowing Chuck wouldn't be yelling at her every move.

At the end of senior year, there was a graduation ceremony for all graduating students, even those who would be returning for Grade 13. Because Tracy was headed to Grade 13, Wendy and Chuck didn't attend the ceremony that year. They were the only parents not there.

During that time in her life, her relationship with Chad grew stronger. He became the rock she relied on to get her through the day. The next school year, Prom was held in the spring and of course, he was her date. Tracy was crowned Prom Queen and when she arrived home that night wearing the Prom Queen sash across her dress, Wendy laughed and asked Tracy who she had stolen it from.

Tracy wondered, what had she done to cause Wendy not to love her? She told me she didn't believe someone could love a child and still hurt them as much as Wendy's words hurt her.

Tracy planned to travel through Europe with a girlfriend after graduation, taking a year off from school. But, at the last minute, her friend decided to go to school instead, and Tracy didn't do the traveling she had been looking forward to.

That summer, she got into another altercation with Chuck and Wendy that became physical and bloody. She left the house to ride her bike to Chad's, who lived 13 miles away, but her bike tire went flat so she stuck out her thumb for a ride. A car pulled over with, as Tracy described, a little old man and a little old lady with who, she believed must have been their granddaughters in the back seat. They were traveling right past where she was headed and offered to drop her off. She must have been a bloody sight, the two young girls stared at her the whole time.

When she got to Chad's, she began to contemplate the options she had in her life. She didn't have enough money saved to leave home yet. With nowhere else to go, she vowed that she would save every penny and if there was ever any physical abuse again, that would be it, she would leave home.

Tracy learned that Chad called Chuck and Wendy to tell them that what they had done was unacceptable. During the call, Wendy chastised Chad for having sex with Tracy in their house. Tracy had warned Chad earlier in their relationship that someday, her parents would accuse him of having sex with her under their roof. And when that day comes, to say it's never happened. As they had agreed, he denied it.

Unsuccessful in getting an admission from Chad, Wendy tried to trick Tracy. She told her she had spoken with Chad and that he admitted they had sex under their roof. Tracy replied that she knew exactly what he said. He said no. "No, we haven't, because we haven't."

Tracy's work hours were still part-time and with her plan in mind, she wanted to fill her schedule. She found a job as a waitress at a fine dining restaurant owned by an Italian couple. The tips were fantastic, and she learned so much about the industry from them. But to Chuck and Wendy, working 4 pm to midnight was not a real job. They still expected her to wake early to complete the list of chores each day before she left for work. It was always a struggle.

Tracy smiled as she told me about the day, they asked her to put a pot of chili on the stove to warm for supper. Wendy reminded her to stir it occasionally, which she did, but it still managed to stick to the bottom of the pot and burn a bit. When supper was served, they complained

128

about how burnt it was and asked why she let that happen. They ate something else but made her sit at the table until she finished her burnt bowl of chili, to prove their point. Finally, at 10 pm, when she had neither taken a bite nor stepped away from the table, she was told she could go to bed without supper. She was nineteen.

That fall, her grandparents invited her to spend some time with them on their boat in the south. It was good to get away. She and Chad had briefly parted ways a few weeks prior, so it was nice to have some time on the water to clear her head. By the time she returned home, it was almost Christmas, and everyone was wrapped up in the festivities.

After Christmas, Tracy headed north to look after her cousins while her Aunt and Uncle went on a holiday. She wasn't spending much time at home, which was a good thing. When she did return home, she was told how peaceful things were when she wasn't there.

Soon after, Chuck spun out of control again. Tracy had promised herself that would be the last straw - and it was. She left that day and never lived with them again.

Over the next seven years, she put herself through university, moved a dozen or so times, and met her now-husband, Trevor.

The summer after Tracy graduated from university, they celebrated her grandparents' 50th wedding anniversary. Some of the family asked what was next for her and Trevor and she told them they planned to move in together. Upon hearing the news, Wendy asked Trevor when he was planning to ask their permission. Tracy hadn't had much of a relationship with them since she'd left home. And, in her opinion, they had no right to assume they had any say in what she did.

Distance with Wendy and Chuck continued to grow.

She remembered the first time she and Trevor invited his parents for dinner. Trevor's mom, Mary, offered to bring a pie. It was all set. But Chuck and Wendy happened to call to see what their plans were for the night. Tracy told them Trevor's parents were coming for dinner. And then, to fill the awkward silence that ensued, Tracy blurted out what she thought Wendy wanted to hear, asking if they'd like to come for dinner too. Wendy accepted the invite and offered to bring pie. Tracy knew from experience it was better to accept than to argue. She hung up the phone and immediately dialed Trevor's mom, who offered to bring something else. She also brought the pie which they hid in the cupboard to be safe. Mary was familiar with Tracy and Wendy's history. Wendy brought pie and the pie hiding in the cupboard was never spoken of until she shared the story with me.

After renting for a year, Tracy and Trevor decided it would be better for them financially to be homeowners. During that first year, Trevor had been commuting an hour and a half to and from work six nights a week. He applied for jobs in their area and was soon hired as an Assistant Quality Manager at an automotive parts manufacturer. For them, it was a far cry from where he had been just three and a half years prior and Tracy was fiercely proud of how far he'd come.

Tracy told me about a phone conversation with Wendy during which she announced that she didn't think things were going well between the three of them, Chuck, Wendy, and Tracy. Tracy reminded her of the abuse she had endured as a child. Wendy told her, "Everything you got you deserved." The declaration shocked Tracy. She couldn't have disagreed more. She responded, "But I was the kid, you were the adults. You were supposed to protect and teach me." The conversation deteriorated from there and when Tracy hung up the phone, she told me she had known it would be a long time before they spoke again.

Tracy refused to allow the unhealthiness of that relationship to spill into the great new life she had been working so hard to build. She set some firm boundaries and without the negative speak that only came from Chuck and Wendy, her life was gloriously happy.

The boundaries she had set that day lasted for a few years. Her interaction with Chuck and Wendy was extremely limited. It gave her time to grow into the person she desired to be, not who they expected her to be. She had walked away from their agenda once before but acknowledged she may need to do it again.

At that time, her job in recruitment involved opening new retail locations which took ten days per new store. In the first two days, she would teach the management team the entire recruitment process. Then in the eight days that followed, they would host a three-day job fair, conduct two days of interviewing, followed by two days of reference checking, and finally one day of job offers. After those ten intense days, they would have hired one hundred new employees to open the new location.

After the second day of intense training, Tracy arrived home, exhausted. Waiting for her, just like every other night, was their first cat, Fergus, a big orange furball. She picked him up, gave him his usual kiss but as she set him back down, she noticed something hanging around his neck. It was a jewelry box. As she started to untie the ribbon, she wondered where Trevor was. Once the box was open, Trevor appeared from around the corner and asked for her hand in marriage. She said YES, with tears in her eyes. He then surprised her with a steak dinner that he had prepared and a bottle of chianti.

Before they sat down to eat, they called Trevor's parents. Trevor's mom answered and Tracy informed her that her son had asked her to marry him. Tracy giggled when she recalled Mary's response. "When?" Trevor's parents were genuinely happy for them to be taking this next step in their lives.

The next phone call was to Tracy's aunt and uncle, with whom she had a close relationship. Of course, they were thrilled. They loved Trevor.

Tracy doesn't know how or when Wendy and Chuck learned about their engagement. She told me she had long ago let go of the hope that theirs would ever be the loving, normal parent-child relationship she'd envisioned as a child.

Tracy and Trevor were married the following May. They chose a beautiful venue on the lake for their mini-destination wedding. They were the first grandchildren on at least two sides to get married, so instead of an island destination wedding, they compromised and held it close enough for everyone to drive.

Shortly after their engagement, her grandmother had asked who she was going to have in her wedding party. Her list did not include her half-sister, Lori, and her grandmother questioned the omission. Tracy told her that the people she wanted to ask were those who she loved and respected, who were her go-to people on a daily basis. Her grandmother knew that Lori did not fit that category, but still insisted. Tracy told her it wasn't going to happen. Her grandmother worried if she didn't have Lori in her wedding party, that her parents may never speak to her again. That was a risk Tracy was willing to take.

Once Wendy finally heard they were getting married, she called to ask what she could do. Tracy told them everything was taken care of. She and Trevor were paying for everything themselves, primarily so she didn't feel the need to ask permission for any of their decisions. The only thing she told Wendy she needed to do was choose the color of dress that she would wear. Mother-of-the-Bride traditionally gets first pick, and Tracy at least wanted to honor that. Then, the Mother-of-the-Groom would choose followed by Tracy's dad's wife.

Each month as the wedding drew nearer, Trevor's mom asked if Wendy had chosen a color and each time, Tracy had to tell her that she hadn't heard. Tracy thinks it was about six weeks before the wedding when she called Wendy for the last time to ask what color she was wearing. She still hadn't fully decided, so Tracy asked what color she thought she might wear. Her answer was periwinkle blue. Tracy told her she had to go with that color so she could tell the other moms.

Wendy had her dress made yet was still working on the hem the morning of the wedding. What bothered Tracy most about that was her mother had no other responsibility for their wedding, just her dress, and she left it to the last minute. For Tracy, it was very clear how important this wedding was to her.

The night before the wedding, their rehearsal went as planned. Everyone in the wedding party, along with Tracy and Trevor's families were invited to a post-rehearsal dinner. Their suite was large enough to host thirty people for dinner and provided more than enough room for Tracy and her bridesmaids to sleep there that night.

At the end of the dinner, Chuck and Wendy decided it was a good time to present their wedding gift. Tracy rolled her eyes as she recounted this part of the story, acknowledging her parents' need for public validation. As Trevor and Tracy opened the parcel, there were a ton of oohs and aahs at the handiwork inside - a beautiful quilt, made with white and tan colored fabric, in a pattern called Drunkard's Path. Chuck and Wendy had spent the previous few weeks working madly on creating this gift for them.

It was a wonderful gesture, but to this day, when Tracy sees the quilt, it's a slap in the face. It is a stark reminder from when she was young. Wendy had purchased a raffle ticket, the prize a handmade quilt in the Drunkard's Path pattern, made with white and hot pink fabric. It was bold. And Tracy loved it. It didn't match with any of their house decor, so you would typically find it on the end of her bed. She has photos from sleepovers with her girlfriends, all cuddled under that blanket. That quilt for Tracy was like Linus with his blanket, well into her teen years.

When she left home, she asked for one thing - that blanket. Her request was met with a resounding 'No'. And then, when visiting Wendy and Chuck a few years later, the blanket was rolled up in the dog bed. It was good enough for the dogs but not for her. I could see that would always be a sore spot for her.

Ouch. I could see why that would feel like a complete slap in the face for her. I continued to see the toxic pattern she was forced to navigate when it came to her parents and I had hopes that as the years progressed, we'd see a level of maturity take hold. She promised her list of stories would be exhausted by the end of our next session.

CHAPTER 12

Cathy: The Other Woman

When Cathy was five, her parents split for the final time. She told me matter-of-factly that her mom got custody with no questions asked. Her dad was only twenty-eight when he became newly single, still very young. Gradually, he'd started dating again. When Cathy was about seven, he met Joanne. Each time she visited him, they would all spend a little more time with each other. Eventually, Joanne and her dad moved in together.

For Cathy, this was awesome. She loved Joanne. The three of them used to sit together in bed at night and watch movies and eat big bowls of popcorn. This was as close to a happy family as she'd ever experienced, and she loved the weekends she spent with them.

Joanne was not shy about her feelings, that she didn't especially like kids, or that she had never wanted any children of her own. She did, however, admit that Cathy had grown on her, and had shown her that kids, too, had personalities - if you gave them a chance. Over time, Cathy and Joanne formed a close bond, one that Cathy knew made her dad happy.

Over time, Cathy's relationship with Joanne grew even stronger. Returning home from her weekend visits with her dad, Joanne was all she could talk about. She knows now that her mom hated it, but as a kid, she didn't understand or realize that talking about Joanne would irk her mom so much.

When Cathy was twelve, her dad was granted permission to take her on a two-week vacation to Florida. She was 1600 miles from home, the farthest she'd ever been at that point in her life. Halfway through the trip, Joanne flew down to join them. During that second week in Florida, Cathy remembers feeling some tension growing between herself and Joanne for the first time, ultimately coloring her memories of that trip. Even now, she vividly recalls, in her twelve-year-old excitement, repeatedly asking when they were getting to Disneyworld. After a few days of her eager questioning, Joanne had snapped at Cathy like never before. "We'll get there when we get there! Do NOT ask again." In that simple instant, her childhood excitement at the prospect of Disney was extinguished, never to return. The hurt I saw flash in Cathy's eyes was unmistakable, all these years later.

Cathy described the three of them trying to decide where to eat one night. She grimaced at how vocal they all were about their own preferences and the recollection of her dad going crazy trying to listen to everyone. As the hope of group consensus dwindled in reverse correlation to his rising impatience, he quickly turned the steering wheel, pulling into the nearest parking lot, not caring what he found. As Cathy got out of the car, she happened to look through the window of the restaurant they'd parked in front of, paying particular attention to the people sitting at the booth inside. This, Cathy explained to me, was when it first dawned on her just how small the world really was. As it turned out, the man in the booth was one of her stepfather's best friends from back home, dining with his wife. She went in and said hello, and of course, introduced them to her dad and Joanne. All these years later, Cathy can still remember how awkward she felt during that whole interaction.

In discussion, Cathy shared some observations with me. Had she been a little older at the time of the trip, she said she might have noticed the level of friction between her dad and Joanne, correlating it to some of the tension she'd also been feeling. But, at the time, she couldn't have known. Cathy was accustomed to conditions of overt tension and daily bickering in her own home, courtesy of her mother and stepfather. By comparison, her dad and Joanne had still seemed to be madly in love. She had chalked it up to not sleeping in their own beds and the long, hot days in the sun.

The day she learned the truth, Cathy told me, is one she'll never forget. She was fourteen when her mom hung up from a call with Cathy's uncle, her mom's younger brother. He still made regular business trips to the town where her dad and Joanne lived. Her mom had immediately come to share the news with Cathy, that her dad and Joanne had split up. Even as she struggled to process the information, she could sense a palpable, albeit subconscious joy coming from her mother and struggled to make sense of this observation. Cathy was crushed. She was crushed because they were no longer together. She was crushed because she knew she would really miss Joanne. She was crushed because she would miss seeing her dad happy with Joanne. But most of all, she was crushed because she'd had to hear the news through the grapevine.

With age, of course, comes wisdom, and with wisdom comes clarity. In retrospect, Cathy understands why it's no surprise that her dad didn't pick up the phone and tell her the news himself. She knows that he doesn't do well with tough conversations today, and that he didn't do any better with them back then, either.

Despite her split from Cathy's father, Joanne and Cathy stayed in touch over the years, mostly around birthdays and holidays. Cathy is comforted by the fact that Joanne will always be very special to her, and that she has an indelible place in both her history and her heart. She played a huge role in Cathy's life for more than seven years and Cathy will never forget the love she showed her during that time. Unfortunately, once Cathy's dad remarried, he asked her to never mention Joanne's name again in front of his new wife. When pressed to explain, he told Cathy that the flack he had to deal with whenever Joanne's name was mentioned just wasn't worth it. His new wife had a streak of insecurity and this was not a good topic.

A few months before her own wedding, Cathy received a call from her dad, asking if Joanne would be invited to the wedding. Only somewhat surprised, and entirely undeterred, Cathy told him that in fact, yes, she was. When he tried to explain why he didn't think it was a good idea, she told him she was inviting people to her wedding who she loved and who she wanted to witness her exchange vows on their special day. Joanne was one of those people. Equally undeterred, Cathy's dad repeated his assertion that it wasn't a good idea, and she reiterated that Joanne was on the guest list. She described how her father paused for a moment, presumably gathering his thoughts, before he said, "If you invite her to the wedding, I won't give you any money towards it." Although her dad and his wife had promised a few thousand dollars to help towards the cost, having Joanne attend her wedding would be priceless. She calmly and firmly ended the conversation telling her dad to keep his money.

Cathy was furious, but if she was honest with herself, she wasn't surprised. She struggled to beat back the self-pitying questions that started to enter her mind, but it was difficult to do. Why had she been saddled with parents whose personal agendas were always more important than hers, even when it came to her own wedding?

In the spirit of acknowledging victories, no matter how small, Cathy's dad did call back a few weeks later. He told her that he'd given it a lot of thought and that she was right. It was her wedding after all, and she had the right to invite whoever she wanted to be part of the special day. That had been her plan all along.

Now, let's put things in perspective. At the time of her wedding, Cathy explained to me that Joanne had been in a long-term relationship and was not going to be out on the prowl. In fact, Joanne and her partner already had plans to fly out west that weekend, so attending the ceremony would be a quick detour for them. They couldn't even stay for the reception, which probably worked out best for everyone. Most important for Cathy was the fact that Joanne got to be there to see her say "I Do" first-hand and how happy the bride was on her wedding day.

When Cathy's first child was born, she waited six full weeks before calling Joanne to share the news. This was not a reflection of any growing distance between the two women, but rather, evidence of Cathy's desire to be respectful of her dad's wishes. Shortly after sharing the good news with her, Joanne was in Cathy's neck of the woods and arranged to pay her a visit, to meet her new bundle of joy.

A few days after she'd visited Cathy and her newborn, Joanne unexpectedly ran into Cathy's dad's wife at an event back home. They were friendly, saying hello and exchanging pleasantries, before she'd asked Joanne if she'd heard about Cathy's new addition. Joanne told her that, yes, she had heard the news, and mentioned that she'd even been able to visit a few days earlier. At this point in the story, Cathy rolled her eyes, an expression of exasperation crossing her face momentarily. "The shit I got because of that," she remembers. She went on to relate what followed, how her father confronted her yet again, following his wife's exchange with Joanne. This time, he was calling to tell his daughter that it would be best that she have no further contact with Joanne moving forward. In other words, he told Cathy to cut Joanne out of her life entirely, as if she'd never been part of it at all.

Sitting in front of me, Cathy threw her arms up in despair. She knew that finally, that year, she would need to make a tough decision about how to move forward. On one side of the coin, her dad was her dad and she didn't want to unnecessarily cause any undue hardship in his life. But really, to be banned from talking to Joanne because of someone else's insecurities, Cathy wasn't comfortable playing into that hand. Each option certainly had its drawbacks.

I helped Cathy examine her current status in life. She was a successful adult with a family of her own, yet her dad still insisted on trying to control her life in certain areas. She was a smart, confident woman, who, after reviewing all pertinent factors, was capable of making choices in her own best interest.

In this case, Cathy could not see the justification in severing a long-standing relationship simply to satisfy the juvenile behavior being thrust in her face. She certainly wouldn't make grandiose efforts to engage with Joanne, but she decided right there and then that she would not eliminate her entirely from her life.

CHAPTER 13

Stephanie: Her Can of Worms

My conversations with Stephanie weren't long ones. Nor did it seem agonizing for her to share personal information when she did. That was her personality. She got straight to the point and rarely overanalyzed situations. Until later.

This discussion had started no differently. She didn't elaborate much. She didn't divulge a lot of information. I learned that Stephanie hadn't ever previously shared many of the details she was about to confide in me. Bits and pieces had been told to a select few over the years, but only her husband knew the bulk of the story.

The abuse began when she was young, seven or eight years old, and continued for three or four years. She doesn't exactly remember the timing and would prefer not to. Back then, Stephanie didn't tell anyone what was going on. She was too ashamed. It had begun the way that this type of abuse usually starts, with conversations about sex; how much she knew, what she had done. At that age, she laughed, it wasn't much.

It was encouraging to see, in her laughter, that she had a light perspective about the whole situation.

Because the abuse was dark. Full and complete penetration every time they were alone together; mornings, afternoons, evenings. It didn't matter the time of day. There wasn't any way she could avoid it, so it became easier for her to let him have his way and get on with her day. When she was easily agreeable, he would leave her alone, until the next time.

And there was always a next time. My heart was breaking for Stephanie, not only for what she had endured, but for the fact that her childhood and her innocence had been stolen from her, and at such a young age.

As she recounted those early events in her life, I witnessed her struggle just once. I would soon learn that Stephanie's story was even more complicated than I had originally perceived. For reasons that were beyond her control, Stephanie's abuser was someone she would continue to encounter for many years after the abuse began.

She was still reluctant to share many details. She did describe the disgust and impatience he exhibited each time she arrived wearing her apparel of choice; overalls. Easy access was impeded by the extra unbuckling of straps and subsequent clothing removal.

Stephanie finally, but hesitantly described a pivotal event when he asked her to follow him into the bathroom. Walking down the hall, she anticipated him taking advantage of her in his usual way, with everyone else out of earshot. But as she opened the door, there, on the floor in front of the sink, lay another male, naked from the waist down, whom she immediately recognized. Stephanie told me that she will never forget the image of him in the bright lights of the bathroom. Lying there with his penis fully erect, he searched her eyes, expecting her to willingly partake in the same activities that her abuser must have described to him. She admitted that was the first time she found the courage to turn around and run away. As disgusted as she was by that vivid memory, she described the fortitude that grew inside her that night, empowering her to refuse all future advances. It was definitely a turning point.

Throughout her childhood and teenage years, Stephanie lived in self stipulated silence regarding her abuse. She frequently found herself doing a double-check for symptoms, but thankfully, none had emerged.

Years later, she confronted her abuser in the parking lot of a bar they'd all been drinking at. She had been trying to understand the motivation behind what he'd done to her, so she came right out and asked him – Why?

His response was the one thing she couldn't have anticipated.

He apologized. He said he didn't know why he had done it and admitted the memories had haunted him for years. He cried like a baby and begged Stephanie for her forgiveness.

Calling on strength that most of us will never have to forge, Stephanie somehow accepted his apology. She chose to believe in the depth of his remorse, and forgave him on the spot, promising that she would never reveal his identity.

At that point in her story, Stephanie stated very confidently that she is completely at peace with this part of her past. I asked her how she knew. She told me that she has an incredibly hard time forgiving people for things they have done when they should have known better. But she remembers in that moment, standing in the gravel parking lot in the dark, feeling complete and utter forgiveness.

She shared that in her years of reflection, she continues to reaffirm that his actions haven't affected her in the long run in the least. She believes the ease with which she forgave him is the reason. She told me that as an adult, she's always enjoyed healthy relationships, never experiencing issues with intimacy or trusting people. She exudes high self-esteem and confidence. She never experienced the typical symptoms of sexual abuse. And until that year, she didn't believe any had emerged.

It's ironic how the awful abuse of her childhood circled back to haunt her. Stephanie admitted that the reason it resurfaced was as a result of her own mother. She told me that about twenty years ago, she had a phone conversation with her mom's mom. Her grandmother had shared with her that her mom wasn't in a very good place at the time; that she was struggling with issues from her past. Her grandmother had divulged to Stephanie that her mom had been sexually abused as a young child and had never had the chance to deal with it. Her grandmother suggested that it might be a good idea for Stephanie to give her mom a call.

From past conversations, I knew that Stephanie and her mother shared a strained relationship, so I was curious to hear what happened next.

Stephanie exclaimed that it was the last thing she could ever fathom talking to her mother about, but she called anyway. She told her mom that she'd had a conversation with her grandmother and was wondering how she was doing. Her mom was a little shocked that such personal information had been shared but went on to admit that it had happened a very long time ago. As was all too common, it had been one of her father's friends. The sad part was when she'd attempted to tell her parents about it, they hadn't believed her. Instead, they locked her secret in a closet, where Stephanie's mother had kept it hidden and eating away at her all these years.

How do you respond to that admission? I couldn't imagine how I'd react to a story like this, and Stephanie admitted that she'd had no idea, either. She wound up choosing the first thing that came to her mind, which was, "I know how you feel". She told me that her mother was aghast and retorted with, "How the hell would you know how it feels?" That was when Stephanie revealed to her, for the first time, that it had happened to her, too.

Her mother's knee-jerk and not atypical response was to accuse her of lying. She then immediately demanded to know who it was. But Stephanie said she'd never tell. "He apologized." She added, "And I forgave him on the spot. It hasn't affected my life."

The next words that her mother spoke are ones that Stephanie still catches herself playing over in her head. "Don't kid yourself," she said. "You've got a can of worms inside of you and some day, when you least expect it, it's going to burst open. You just wait."

Stephanie sadly recalls shaking her head in the moment, only a tiny bit surprised at her mother's reaction. She'd become used to most things being turned around to ensure her mother was the center of attention, but considering the topic, it left her feeling raw. Deep down, a very small part of her wished her mother could step out of the situation for just one moment to acknowledge the horror of what had happened to her daughter. Stephanie laughed at herself and wondered how she could still expect a typical motherly response after all the years of its absence.

That's why Stephanie came to talk to me that year. With the residual effect from her mother's comments, she found herself continually doing that double-check, even years later. Those words have haunted her. She regularly felt the need to look over her shoulder, to ensure those worms weren't crawling up behind her. Despite her wisdom and the self-confidence that she worked hard to rebuild in the aftermath of the abuse, her mother's words still loitered in her head. She wondered how this long-ago uttered threat, one born from her mother's own pain, continued to have such a profound effect.

While it didn't happen right away, Stephanie ultimately made the decision to stop this cycle of self-questioning.

As our conversation progressed, I was finally able to grasp more about the whole situation. Our discussion helped her come to terms with the way her mother's words had introduced fear into her own life. Stephanie eventually told me that she knew she was the only one who could stop it in its tracks. She was the only one who could change the tape playing on repeat in her head. "Enough is enough!" she had said.

After all the years she'd spent questioning herself, Stephanie acknowledged the benefit of sharing the whole story with someone, from start to finish. She had finally reached that point of vulnerability. Stephanie acknowledged, in no uncertain terms, that she ultimately accepted the issues her mother was projecting were just that, her mother's issues.

She recognized that she'd already been able to deal with the past, and that without the noise from her mother, that's where it all would have remained. The cathartic healing that sharing her story provided was just the antidote she needed to understand fully how to move forward. Her own issues had been dealt with. The only question she now faced was how to ensure her mother's words would never tear her soul apart again.

At the end of our conversation, Stephanie admitted that she finally had the courage she required to move forward confidently. She had identified the factors that were important to her. She didn't believe this dark topic would come up with her mother again. It was no longer an option that she would entertain. And she knew that if it did happen, she would be prepared to deflect the pain and let her mother know, in no uncertain terms, that she should focus solely on dealing with her own can of worms.

CHAPTER 14

Rebecca (Part 2): Second-Guessing

As I reviewed my notes before Rebecca's upcoming appointment, I circled back to the tough decisions she'd been forced to make as a kid. As much as her story saddened me, I was hopeful that her parents' divorce and subsequent upbringing had somehow had a positive effect in helping sculpt her into the strong woman she'd become.

We dove right in where we'd left off, with Rebecca in reflection about her childhood, wishing there had been someone to reach out and hug. Because her parents presented such a perfect façade to the outside world, no one knew what was really going on behind closed doors. She felt very alone as a kid, which carried throughout all her teen years. She didn't feel like she had anyone she could talk to. I told her I thought that was a really sad statement. She thinks that's why, as a parent now, she's overly cognizant of maintaining open lines of communication with her kids. At a very early age, she was already long gone from building any type of relationship with her parents.

She continued to take the bus to visit her Dad, usually every third or fourth weekend. On Saturdays, it was their ritual to visit her grandparents and then her Aunt Shirley and Uncle Henry. Her cousin, Katherine, played the flute and they always stole away for a rendition of "Puff, the

Magic Dragon". When she was still very young and it was time for bed, they used to push the boys' twin beds together, with her sleeping in between. She lovingly referred to it as sleeping "On The Crack", one of her greatest memories with her cousins. Regardless of her age, she always felt loved and accepted for who she was with her aunt and uncle. Those weekends with her Dad were always special. She was well aware that he tried to make up a month's worth of time in a weekend with her. He didn't know exactly how to do that except with money. He would buy her things and take her out to eat. Invariably, he sent her home with a 50 dollar bill in her wallet. That never went over well with Charlene. More than once, Rebecca was told that she was a different person when she got home and that things were much more peaceful when she wasn't around. It was always such a stark contrast to the love and warmth she felt from her Dad.

Rebecca told me that it was much later in life before she learned most of what actually transpired between her parents leading up to their divorce. Ryan was a lineman with the local power company. To become a lineman, your training consisted of working for six months each in four different cities, requiring completion of two years of training before becoming fully certified.

Rebecca always described her dad as kind and generous. It was no surprise when the next batch of linemen trainees arrived in town, to find her dad offering their spare room. There was one young man who still hadn't found a local apartment.

That is how Len came to live with them. As Rebecca has previously recounted, Charlene and Ryan had already been having problems and fought every day. At the time, Rebecca was fairly oblivious to what was actually going on. She doesn't know how long he lived with them but has vague memories of visiting his apartment in town, a place he must have lived after moving out of their house. She also remembers visiting him with her mom in another town where he must have gone for his next six months of training. This was during warm weather months and just her with her mom, so she couldn't have been older than four or five at the time.

As the puzzle pieces started to fall into place, Rebecca figured out her mom became pregnant with Len's baby while they were still living with her dad. Rebecca learned later that people congratulated her dad on the birth of his son. He thanked them without explanation, so as not to rock the boat. He was too nice to say anything. She said she couldn't imagine what he must have been going through on the inside.

Once Len had finished his training and moved back to his hometown, he and Rebecca's mom bought a house together. That was the house they moved into the day her short little life was abruptly turned upside down.

Rebecca vaguely recalled her first meeting with Len's family, describing it as pretty surreal. It marked the underlying current of energy that she would feel around them throughout her childhood. She knows now that it started with how Len felt towards her, even though she doesn't believe there will come a time when he will acknowledge his true feelings. If she wasn't truly accepted by him, how could the rest of his family embrace her?

During that first meeting, where this now five-month-old adorable baby, Steven, was being passed around and cooed over, Rebecca found herself standing invisibly in the back corner observing the scene. A man and woman approached her and introduced themselves. They were in their early twenties and were the first people to seem genuinely interested in her. They were Len's older brother, Troy, and his new wife, Lucy. Little did she know at the time the impact they would have on her the rest of her life.

They tried, they really did, Len and Charlene. They read book after book about how to raise children. Rebecca and her brother were raised in a very strict household, so their manners were impeccable, and they never spoke out of turn in public. If they misbehaved in a restaurant, they were silently grabbed by the upper arm and dragged away to the nearest washroom or corner for a spanking. They were told they could return to the table when they thought they could behave.

Anyone looking at their family from the outside was never given a glimpse of the complete dysfunction on the inside. The maintenance of a squeaky-clean reputation was paramount in their home. Unbeknownst to her at the time, Rebecca had started creating a subconscious checklist as to how she would approach her own life and what her marriage would need to look like. She never wanted her home to be anything like the one she grew up in. From an early age, she worked hard at self-awareness and promised herself, when she finally said yes, they would have already built a foundation for marital success.

Rebecca doesn't know how old she was when the reality of how ostracized she felt from her families fully struck her. She thinks maybe it was after she found her own peace. Each of her parents had remarried and become focused on those added responsibilities, including the additional children that resulted.

Rebecca fought to belong, but it wasn't meant to be. She was always someone's baggage. For Len, she was a reminder of Charlene's relationship with Ryan. And for her dad's second wife, Nita, she was a reminder of his relationship with Charlene. As much as anyone could have hoped for a modicum of maturity and selflessness, it proved to be a lose-lose situation for Rebecca.

Her eyes clouded over as she told me about the time she went back to visit Charlene and Len shortly after she'd moved out. There, proudly displayed on their wall, was a family portrait of the four of them. Charlene and Len and Rebecca's half-brother and half-sister, looking pleased as punch. Rebecca felt like she'd been sucker-punched. That was the final nail in the coffin.

Despite Rebecca's childhood, she has experienced such joy as a result of many of the choices she's made. And when the time came, her wedding couldn't have been more perfect. Rebecca had debated forever about who would walk her up the aisle. Everyone suggested that she have both Len and Ryan, one on each arm. But that didn't sit well with her for a few reasons. She could only picture the sheer awkwardness of having one of them on each side, confining both arms. How would she hold her bouquet? What about the train of her dress? She had pictured a comedy of errors. She thought long and hard about including her stepfather, Len. Although he'd been around for years at that point in her life, she didn't feel he deserved to be on her arm. They weren't in a very good place with each other. And then there was her father, Ryan. Things were okay with him but not perfect. If anyone should have been walking Rebecca up the aisle, it most certainly should have been him. But she knew that if Ryan walked her up the aisle and Len didn't, it would have severed her relationship with Len forever. At that point, she wasn't yet prepared for that. So, she chose no one. She was a strong, independent woman who had created an awesome life for herself, allowing no one else to take any credit for the person she'd become. I asked her if she'd ever had regrets about that decision. She divulged that there were certainly times when she felt that perhaps ignoring Len's sensitivity and honoring Ryan with that privilege might have been a better choice. I let her sit with that.

When Rebecca had shared the news of walking up the aisle alone with some friends, they suggested that maybe she have a backup plan in case she woke up that morning feeling like she could use some support. She thought her brother, Steven, would prove to be the perfect person to lean on so she called him and shared her thoughts. He was honored to be a stand-in if necessary. But, as it turned out, there was no need for concern. She felt more at ease and peace with herself on her wedding day than she had in a long time. She was making her own decisions and choices with her new husband, Scott, from there on out, no one else could intervene. So she thought.

Rebecca laughed as she told me about the time she and Scott first started discussing kids. She wanted six. And he thought she was crazy. When people asked her why six, she said it was because when she was ten, Charlene had her sister, her other aunt had twins and another aunt had triplets, six kids all within six months of each other. She had grown up with lots of babies around her and knew that was her happy place.

Once Scott agreed to have kids, he admitted to only wanting two. He always wanted at least one parent to be there for whatever the kids had going on. If one had a game and the other a concert, they'd be able to divide and conquer, and the kids would always know they were equally important. Rebecca respected his point of view and subsequently, they made a deal. They'd have two kids and then evaluate where things stood. She started looking at what she knew. She'd grown up in a household with five people. It was then that she realized the world was really made for four; hotel rooms, restaurant seating, cars unless you wanted someone squished in the middle. Many thoughts of how she'd had to adjust all her life with an odd-numbered family came flooding through. Well, however many they had, she preferred to keep it at an even number.

When their second child arrived, Rebecca didn't feel like anything was missing. She felt at peace. It was a contented state of mind, and she knew that was exactly where she needed to be in life. Her family became her soft place to fall. When the world outside was crashing down on her, she found her ultimate solace between their four walls.

Smiling, she shared another story with me. Just as she was hanging up from a lengthy and unresolved "discussion" with their phone company, her twelve-year-old came into her office and said, "Mom, go have a nice warm bath and let it take all of your cares away." Who could refuse an offer like that? Scott was out at volleyball, so it was just her and the kids at home. When she got out of the tub, they came in her room and folded clothes together while watching another episode of their favorite "Gilmore Girls." The next morning, she woke with a bright smile on her face, knowing that without the love and tenderness of her family, the night prior would have turned out a lot differently.

They've learned what makes each other tick. And true to their goals, Scott and Rebecca have spent as much time and money as they can spare, traveling around the world with their kids. Rebecca had recently been judged for that, too. She told me that Charlene commented on how often they traveled with their kids. As Rebecca acknowledged that they did travel extensively, Charlene countered with, "Well, you just didn't take your kids on vacation back when you were growing up." At that point in her life, Rebecca was used to Charlene making excuses and simply shrugged. She knew Charlene was referring to the two trips she and Len had taken each and every year without their kids. That had been their choice, and not as Charlene was projecting, something people just didn't do. Rebecca stepped out of her story and said, "You got to choose what you did and didn't do with your family," I know Rebecca is not one to let people off the hook in blaming society.

Rebecca grinned as she reminisced about booking their family's Mediterranean Cruise. It was so easy to give out her credit card number for that trip. She told the agent on the phone, that she didn't have the countertop in her kitchen that she'd been longing for, but this was going to be some adventure. Rebecca said that the cost of this trip would have covered putting granite throughout her entire house instead. The lady's words still made Rebecca smile. "Oh, Dear, you have all the time in the world for granite countertops and only a short window with your kids. You made the right choice."

So their house isn't too fancy. But have they taken some trips. From their gondola ride in Venice to their helicopter ride over an active volcano in Hawaii, from living in a treehouse 200 feet up in the jungles of Belize to the Olympics in Vancouver, they definitely have some favorites, and they have all been memorable. They all love to reminisce and look back fondly at old pictures.

Rebecca will never stop traveling with her kids as long as they'll join her, she says. They've talked to friends who have older kids who have started taking their kids' significant others with them. They had discussed this as a good compromise once the kids get older. And then they met this pair of early twenty-something sisters on a sunny afternoon on the island of Caye Caulker. They talked about how they had traveled extensively with their family growing up and that this was one of the first times they'd traveled alone. Rebecca joked to them that, as parents, they'd have to keep upping the ante with locations so the kids would still want to come. They asked the girls what they did through their teenage years. They said that there had been a few holidays when they'd been allowed to bring their boyfriends. But, in looking back, they certainly weren't the best memories. They talked about the pictures, and how, now that they'd moved on, it was sometimes awkward going through trip photos with new boyfriends. They talked about how they finally realized that the best trips were just family. Rebecca was so thankful that her kids were in earshot when they gave their answer.

That's how Rebecca thought she felt. But with the little nudges she'd received from Charlene over the years, she was starting to question everything. That, coupled with the lack of any relationship example having been set for her, she was really marching forward blindly. Why did she think her way was best? Maybe her parents had been good role models after all. Who knew if what she was doing would actually cause negative side effects for her kids down the road? Her mind was spinning with the possibility that what she thought was right, was perhaps completely wrong.

As I sat watching her work herself into a bit of a frenzy, I could see why she needed to talk. I asked her to sit back in her chair, as she'd inched forward bit by bit in retelling her stories. I told her to relax all of her muscles, including the clenched ones she was probably sitting on. That made her smile. I asked her to relax her hands on the armrests and take a few deep breaths.

As she did that, I started asking her questions. They centered around the reasons why she'd made certain decisions in her life and what factors she'd taken into consideration. I asked her, if she could go back, if she would have chosen any other options. She thought a long time on that and other than the walking up the aisle situation, she seemed proud of the majority of decisions in her life.

I asked her about her husband, her kids, were they well-adjusted, did they do well in school, what did they do for fun? She talked about their marks and their sports and their volunteering efforts. But most of all, she talked about how blessed she was as a mom and a wife, living the life she had.

My final question became almost redundant at that point, but I asked Rebecca anyway. "Why are you second-guessing yourself?" She acknowledged that the old tapes had started playing again in her head. She told me that she was scared. She was scared mostly because things were so good, they were almost too good to be true. Hanging her head, she admitted that she had secretly been spending her days waiting for the bottom to fall out.

She looked up at me at that point, with hope in her eyes, and stated confidently that she knew she was a good mom and wife, that their little family of four was proof. She chided herself for being so silly in all her questioning, worry, and doubts. She told me that our conversations had helped her reset. It was exactly what she'd needed to get on with her superb little life.

CHAPTER 15

Christine (Part 2): Divergence

I must admit, learning about Christine's trip out to her sister's wedding, with all the personalities and draining situations she was faced with, made me feel tired for her just listening to her stories. I was really trying to see the good in her sister and was rooting for a happy ending.

Before leaving for the wedding, Christine and her daughter, Emma, had purchased a slew of green decorations and made sure they'd all packed their St. Paddy's day attire. Two days before their flight, Samantha (bride-to-be and sister) called to see if Christine was busy. She was as busy as any mom trying to get her family of four packed for a week's vacation. Turns out, the place where Samantha was supposed to get Todd (brother)'s gift had fallen through, but she'd been able to find another location. She said that conveniently, it was close to Christine's house. Close was a relative term, as it proved to be an hour's drive north. But what choice were they left with? Emma and Christine made the two-hour round trip to pick up Todd's present.

On the day of the party, it was with big secret smiles that they sent all the kids to Christine's suite to decorate. That night, Brittany (niece)'s realization that she'd been tricked into decorating for her own party was priceless. It was a total success and she remembered seeing a few tears in Todd's eyes. The gift they'd chosen was exactly what he'd wanted. Brittany's gift of money would be put to good use by the almost 15-year-old. And the Frozen backpack and cute outfit they'd chosen for Chelsea (niece) were a hit too, along with the cake with all THREE of their names. Christine told me in retrospect, this was probably the highlight of the entire trip. Samantha's husband-to-be, Tim, also made it to the party so the entire family was all together. He'd been pretty non-existent up until then.

Meanwhile, time at the hotel had progressed from bad to worse with requests and demands being made by Samantha to assist with wedding priorities. Christine took it all in stride but confided that it had required her to dig deep into their alcohol stash. Their suite backed onto an open field covered in snow, with garden doors leading to a little patio area and chairs. This was where she told me they'd kept their alcohol cold to free up space in the mini-fridge. On the third day, Kevin (husband) asked if someone might have been stealing their alcohol. As she confessed it was all her, he just shook his head, trying to hide the smile on his face.

Their joint meals were working out better than expected. That was until Patricia and Larry (parents) and Samantha and her family assumed the meals included them too. Todd and Jessica, Kevin and Christine had done all the food planning, shopping - and paying – in order to feed nine people. Adding six more mouths to feed was a stretch. Samantha would text, "Where's breakfast today?" And then she would show up with her kids, plunk them down on the floor and, after giving her breakfast order to whoever was cooking, proceed to spend the entire time on her phone without paying a single mind to her children. It had taken every ounce of will Christine had not to say something. If Samantha's children were well behaved, it might have been a different story. Granted, they were young, but Chelsea had a habit of hitting her brother whenever he did something she didn't like. Bryce had a habit of using a high-pitched squeal about twenty-three hours a day, non-stop. That seemed to be his only form of communication.

Christine had arrived with a full cup, but it was quickly depleting. She was cold, she didn't want to be in the mountains, but most of all, she was tired of witnessing the same behavior from her sister as she had her entire upbringing, with her parents pandering to her every need. It was exhausting. And with late nights and early mornings, her cup was not being replenished. Kevin and Todd took their five kids out on mountain hikes and excursions during the day. They had great fun and came home with awesome memories and pictures. Christine stayed back and helped with wedding preparations - and drank. She looked at me a little worried, saying it sounded as though she had a bit of a problem. She assured me it had stopped as soon as they got back home. I smiled and told her I didn't judge. I gestured for her to continue.

The rest of the week went as Christine had expected, with fires being put out here and there to keep Samantha's ire at bay. The night the boys went out with the groom to celebrate his upcoming nuptials did not end well. The best man was so rowdy and drunk causing such a commotion, that hotel security was called. If he hadn't been part of the wedding party, he would have been kicked out.

If Christine was asked to do something wedding related, she did it. And it seemed like there was something every single day. So, it had surprised Christine when Samantha decided to go snowboarding just a few days before the wedding, leaving her kids with Larry. At one point, he had needed to take care of something, so he asked if Christine would look after Bryce for an hour. The last thing she wanted to do on her "vacation" was look after someone else's kids. He was her nephew, but unfortunately, there wasn't the bond that she had with her other nieces and nephews. Christine begrudgingly watched the clock the entire hour.

In Christine's opinion, Samantha dumped her kids on Larry and Patricia more than they'd ever expected. The kids slept over with them every single night. By the morning after the wedding, Larry and Patricia were so pale and exhausted, she thought they might collapse. She truly felt sorry for them. They had very openly dropped the kids with Tim's mother and said, "Your turn."

Christine admitted to me that even after the tough week she'd endured, the hardest part had been the reception. If being up on the mountaintop in the blowing snow and cold for the ceremony wasn't enough, it was the facade she had to put on for the reception that had really taken its toll. Listening to everyone say such inspiring, nice words about Samantha was sickening for her, especially when it came from Larry and Patricia.

When it came to their emcee responsibilities, it was no surprise that Christine had written the entire speech leaving them only to decide who would read which parts. It went off without a hitch. Christine said Todd had even ad-libbed a bit at one point, boasting that he'd spent hours putting the speech together, prompting the entire audience to roar in laughter.

The next day, two relatives had approached her at separate times asking if she was okay. She'd told them she was fine, but they weren't buying it. She thought she'd been doing a good job disguising her melancholy, but a few close to her could see behind her curtain. She brushed it off as having been a busy week. Truth be told, it had been extremely taxing, and she longed to get away and refill her cup. Christine and her family left later that day and with every mile they covered, her spirits lifted exponentially. It was incredible what a heavy weight she'd been under the entire time she was there. She told me it had taken another four full days at home before she felt like herself again.

Upon her return, a friend familiar with the whole situation asked her why she went to the wedding in the first place. This friend knew Christine to be a pretty resolute person who typically stayed away from all forms of negative energy, whatever the cost. Christine told her enduring that week of hardship was so much easier than the guilt that surely would have been flung in her direction had she not attended. It didn't surprise Christine that there was little interaction with Samantha after the wedding. She attributed the silence to Samantha not needing anything.

Later that fall, Christine was surprised by an unexpected phone call from Samantha. Todd had been conferenced in on another line. Samantha said she had been talking to their dad, Larry. She shared that he was feeling down and lamenting that perhaps he hadn't been a good father or grandfather. Larry had recently discovered some health issues that were perhaps causing some reflection. In calling, Samantha was hoping Christine and Todd would reach out to help make him feel better. There was silence after the request, until Samantha said, "Hello?" Todd replied, "I'm still here," then went on to say he wasn't sure he could do that. He and Larry hadn't seen eye to eye for a few years. Christine told Samantha she understood where she was coming from but that she had a different experience growing up. "I can't tell him he was a good dad or grandfather, because I don't feel that way. I'm sorry, I can't help you." Samantha pressed on saying, "Things are different now. He knows he's sick, he is scheduled to have an additional procedure and who knows what might happen? Why can't you leave all of that in the past?" Christine told her that didn't change her mind, that there was so much she didn't know. Todd added that he shared the same sentiment. Samantha ended the call saying "Okay, I thought I'd try. I get it. Talk to you later." Christine didn't think she got it at all.

As the day of Larry's operation approached, Samantha texted Christine to see when she planned on visiting him in the hospital. Christine knew Samantha would have a hard time understanding why she didn't plan to see him, given she was only 45 minutes away. Samantha lived 2500 miles away and would have done anything to be able to visit him. Christine ultimately told her she wasn't planning to see him, adding that it didn't feel right based on recent interactions with Larry and Patricia.

Shortly after, she received a message from Samantha. This is what it said.

"This will piss you off. And expect that this will put an end to any kind of relationship we've built so far, but I can't not say it. I'm done keeping my mouth shut.

I don't care how fake you think it would feel, you should have the decency to visit the man that tried his best to give you what you needed (even if his best wasn't good enough for you), while he's in the hospital. Your posts about being the better person and learning to forgive are

168

what's fake. You haven't forgiven him or moved on. I'm sick of how selfish you are when it comes to mom and dad. They've screwed up. So what. No one is perfect. Move on. Be an adult. Deal with your issues with them. Go see someone and work through them. I did. I had to. I only have one set of parents and so I had to figure it out. I chose not to be the victim in the situation."

Christine, incredulous at the audacity, had read the text a few times and knew she needed a voice of reason before formulating a reply. She sent Kevin a copy of the text and asked for his thoughts. He pointed out the fact that she and Samantha were raised differently by their parents and had completely opposite relationships with them. He suggested she acknowledge those differences with her sister one last time. Christine messaged Samantha adding that she could have forgiven their behavior if it was in the past, but it continued to that day. She didn't have room for it in her life anymore. Christine proposed that Samantha should go on living her life and that she would go on living hers, but in doing so, their paths probably wouldn't cross. They had such different ways of looking at these things.

Christine never heard back from her and has not spoken with her since, no regrets. She learned that shortly there afterward, Samantha and Tim had called quits on their marriage, not quite eight months in. Christine acknowledged that the underlying issues Samantha was dealing with predicated her emotional behavior but didn't excuse it.

That night, she called her brother, Todd. She had decided that she needed to set firm boundaries with Larry and Patricia and Samantha. And she wanted him to know that she planned to back away from the family as a whole for a while. She told him that she was going to be getting some help to work through her unrest and that she would feel more comfortable talking to him after that was complete. He was furious. He couldn't believe that she had lumped him in with that family. She was sorry, but in her mind, they had always been a package deal.

Christine told him that the way they treated her was unhealthy and there was absolutely no reason why she needed to put up with it anymore. Todd did not agree. She told him again that she would feel better continuing the conversation after she'd had a chance to talk it through with an outside party. It was not a good conversation.

As Christine and I discussed her brother, she acknowledged that lumping him in with the rest of the family seemed harsh in retrospect. Todd and his wife, Jessica, had become allies for the most part in recent years. She'd had the option of maintaining a relationship with them, but she also told me something deep inside her told her it was the right choice.

She admitted to me that she felt like a shell of herself. She felt hollow. She felt like nothing she did mattered. She felt like the decisions she'd made in life were all wrong and were now coming back to haunt her. She had become a tremendously confident wife and mom and yet there she sat, questioning her every move. She realized that the culmination of all her interactions with Larry and Patricia and Todd and Samantha over the past year had taken its toll. She was at an all-time low; the lowest she'd been in decades. She was scared.

As we talked, many questions surfaced. Christine could not understand why Samantha and Patricia insisted on telling her how to act. Every interaction with them pointed out what, according to them, she did or didn't do

170

properly. Why did they feel the need to force their views and opinions on her? Christine certainly didn't agree with everything they did but refused to take every instance as a chance to berate them. Even if Christine had been wearing a suit of armor, it was their modus operandi to pick away until it cracked. They had succeeded.

As Christine started to question if she'd been wrong about her family all of these years and perhaps should have been more accepting, I stopped her. After hearing only bits and pieces of her familial history, I was astounded by what she'd had to put up with. Their behavior stemmed from not dealing with their own litany of issues, but instead projecting and blaming it on others. It became easy to see why they were behaving the way they were but didn't excuse it. We agreed they were their issues, not hers. Christine felt like a huge weight had been lifted. After just one conversation about the recent events, her confidence had returned, and she had renewed hope that she could get through it. She still had some issues that she wanted to work through with me, and final decisions to make about moving forward. We'd planned to meet again the following week.

She texted Todd and Jessica that night to say that we'd spoken but she felt that it would be best for her to get a few more sessions under her belt until she fully stepped back in with family again.

Todd didn't reply, but she did hear back from Jessica who said she respected her wishes and would give her all of the time she needed. During the break in their interaction, her niece had celebrated a birthday. They'd made sure to send a birthday card along with a gift card to her favorite store in recognition of her special day.

Jessica told Christine that Ella was sad that her cousins didn't call on her birthday.

Christine replied to Jessica that this was why she didn't want to communicate. Sharing Ella's disappointment felt like an attempt to make her feel guilty for the actions she deliberately took. She revealed to Jessica that while on the phone with Todd the last time, he had told her she was fucked. With that admission, Christine hoped Jessica could understand why she had chosen to distance herself for a while. Jessica apologized saying it wasn't her intention to make her feel guilty. She sent her love and Christine knew it was genuine.

Christine and I saw each other a few more times and she continued to regain her confidence with each visit. She was comfortable with the decisions she was making about how to move forward and left each time with a smile on her face.

Near the end of November, Christine reached out to Todd to let him know she was in a better place and open to talking again if he was up for that. He texted to let her know he'd be driving home and on the road for a few hours on Sunday night, so that would be a good time.

Christine was encouraged and looking forward to their conversation. That's why she was not at all prepared for what happened next. When they finally got on the phone, his hurt was apparent. She apologized and tried to explain where she was coming from, but his voice grew so loud that she had to hold the phone away from her ear. She told him he was making her feel the way she felt when Larry yelled at her when she was little. He yelled more. She told him she couldn't continue the conversation with him if it was going to be like that. He yelled more... "Oh, we have to put up with your defense mechanism of not talking to us, but you don't have to put up with my defense mechanism, which is yelling?"

And so, Christine listened to him yell. At one point, he was yelling so vehemently she could hear spittle flying out of his mouth. More than once, it reminded her of Larry's temper.

But then he'd turned soft. He acknowledged that he might have said some things out of hurt and apologized. She thought they were making some progress but then he complained about how many times he'd thought of her in the month they hadn't talked. Todd said during that time, that he didn't know if he'd ever have the chance to talk to her again. She said to him that her text had said, maybe after a few more sessions, she'd be in a better place to reach out. He screamed at her, "Maybe, it said maybe. Do you know what that means? M-A-Y-B-E he spelled it out at top volume. Look that up in the fucking dictionary." No one had yelled at her like that in years.

He asked again why she had lumped him in with Larry and Patricia and Samantha when Christine put up walls when he hadn't done anything wrong. She told him that growing up, it always felt like the four of them versus her. Sarcastically he said, "Say that a little sadder," insinuating that she was trying to make him feel sorry for her. She had never heard this kind of talk from her brother. He went on to say that the four of them had always felt that she didn't think they were good enough for her.

She couldn't believe her ears. All her life, Christine had felt like she hadn't been able to ever do anything good enough for them. To hear that they felt she thought she was better than them was mind-boggling. That's when he decided he was tired of the conversation and didn't want it to continue. Christine hasn't heard from him since.

As we dissected their conversation, Christine still couldn't believe how shocked she was at Todd's up and down behavior. It was loud and yelling, then soft and apologetic, then loud and yelling again. She couldn't help but be reminded of a time the previous summer at an amusement park when two guys jumped the line while they were waiting to ride a roller-coaster. Todd had gotten so upset with them, she felt like he'd made it his personal endeavor to make them feel guilty and to stop them from doing it. She had wondered at that time if drug use had crept back into his life after its years of absence. It wasn't a topic she felt she could ever broach with him. There had been a few other incidents over the years since he'd been clean that had made her wonder, and she was wondering again.

As we looked at her options regarding her brother, a few factors rose to the surface. Although she loved him dearly, it was very apparent that his behavior triggered her in a way she wanted no part of. And if he'd slid back into his old ways, you'd never know which Todd you were going to get. Christine admitted that although she was on the mend, her interactions with him had been a set back to her progress each time. She decided right there and then, that until she was completely confident in her ability to deal with him, regardless of his state, she needed to keep her distance.

CHAPTER 16

Maggie: Communication is Key

M aggie and I came to know each other when she was still in her twenties. We spent so much time together over the years, she had become more of a friend than a client. Over coffee one day that *year*, we talked about the first decision we had tackled together, and a few others along the way. We marveled at how far she had come and how confident she now was in her decision-making abilities.

Reaching far back in our memories brought us to a New Year's Eve more than 20 years prior when Maggie was visiting her university friends, Stacey and Angela. They were back in their hometown and headed to a house party to celebrate. She hadn't seen her friends in a while, so she was really looking forward to the inevitable epic night it would no doubt be. She had a bottle of champagne set for midnight, and everyone was to bring a gag gift. After midnight, they would each pick one randomly out of a pile and open it, sure to bring a ton of laughs.

The girls arrived just as the party shifted into full gear. The music was loud. Everyone was having a great time, laughing and drinking and loving life. They were dressed up, too, ready to ring in the new year in style. Maggie remembers wearing a short black silk sequined Leslie Fay dress. Her hair was short at the time and it had been her previous new year's resolution to lose weight. She was feeling good about herself. Maggie had dated a lot that year, and we giggled at some of her memories. There was the classmate who frequently picked her up on his motorcycle, the tall French guy who had professed his love, and the chef she met while working at a resort out west for the summer, who she had talked marriage with. Despite her prolific dating activity, at that time, she was still single.

The clock was about to strike midnight. Everyone was counting down with Dick Clark's New Year's Rockin' Eve. Maggie stood there with her bottle of champagne, struggling to get the cork off. It was something she had done a million times while waitressing over the years. She worried that she wouldn't get it open in time to take her first sip at midnight. Fortunately, a good-looking guy was walking by who looked strong enough to help. Maggie desperately tugged on his sleeve asking for help, and that he be quick about it. He shrugged as he popped the cork on her champagne bottle just as the clock struck midnight. A friend took a picture to capture the moment. And then the handsome stranger disappeared into the sea of people kissing each other to celebrate the new year.

Shortly after midnight, the gag gifts were opened and as anticipated, Maggie's gift provided for quite a few giggles. She settled in by the fireplace enjoying the evening with her friends. And then, she noticed the guy who assisted with her champagne bottle making his way over. Turns out, he was there because he had played ball that summer with the host.

One of their mutual friends proceeded to introduce them properly. His name was Tim. He and Maggie struck up a conversation that lasted hours. It was fun and light and a perfect way to bring in the New Year. It was well after 4 am when the party began to wrap up. Maggie was planning on staying at Angela's house but by then, most of her friends had already made their way home. Tim asked if Maggie needed a ride. Maggie hesitated for a minute and then accepted. He seemed like a decent guy, he was friends with a bunch of people at the party, and Maggie didn't need to be afraid of a short ride home. He said he'd go get his car.

Maggie reminded me of a few details from that night. Tim had gone to university and wore a bright mustard-colored leather school jacket. He also had a head of dark, curly, permed hair. We giggled at the memory. The piece de resistance; he pulled up in a Trans Am. As she leaned down to talk to him through the open window of the passenger door, Maggie vividly remembered asking him, "Are you Italian?" Why he still offered to drive her home escapes her to this day. They chatted for a bit in Angela's driveway and then he leaned in for a kiss. The fireworks that went off must have left a lasting impression.

On their wedding day, five years and four months to the day later, they gave away fireworks as their wedding favor and the note on them said, "Reminiscent of our first kiss." Maggie chuckled at the corniness, but it symbolized the beginning of a long and healthy love story that she is proud to tell.

They lived in towns almost two hours from each other. Maggie did not have a car so their first year of dating was sporadic. Tim worked, mostly weekends, and she attended university full time and worked as well. They spent many hours on the phone and visited as often as they could, but there were times they'd go more than a month without seeing each other. What did it matter anyway? He had told her that he was never getting married and never having kids.

In February of that first year of dating, they were back in Tim's hometown. It was only about six weeks after they met. They had a great time at a party the town hosted each year at the community center complete with a live band and drinks. It was after that party, as Tim kissed her goodnight, that he told her he thought he was falling in love with her. That was a big deal coming from someone who didn't have an easy time sharing his feelings. It was the first time Maggie hadn't made the first move in a relationship in a while.

Since her previous relationships all ended for one reason or another, Maggie decided that she would need to try something new if her relationship with Tim was going to work. Maggie likes to talk about feelings and how things are going, to analyze and speculate. Tim was not a talker. So Maggie thought that maybe she could give his way a shot. For a long time, they didn't talk about if they were dating or not. They didn't talk about the status of their relationship. They just got together when they could and enjoyed each other's company. And it worked, for a while. But then Maggie got antsy. After a year of not knowing what was going on in their "relationship", Maggie finally broached the subject. Maggie guesses it was then that they decided they were dating. Was it exclusive? Maggie doesn't think either of them was sure. With the long-distance thing, it made it hard for them to see each other regularly.

When Maggie met Tim, he was a part-time video clerk in his parents' video store, back when renting VHS movies was a weekend ritual. During one of their long talks, Maggie had asked him what his goals and dreams were.

He talked about finishing university and finding a decent job, instead of what he was doing.

Poor guy. After that conversation, Maggie got on the phone and called ten universities within driving distance of him requesting that each school send a full syllabus to his address. Within a few weeks, these phone books of school courses started arriving at his house. He called her and told her she was crazy. But, eventually, after seventeen years of part-time courses, between working and having kids and buying houses, Tim graduated with a Bachelor of Science in Chemistry. He's a quiet, unassuming guy so he didn't make a big deal of it. But as a family, Maggie said they were so proud of his accomplishment. It was great for him. And it was great to show their kids that if you put your mind to something, it doesn't matter how long it takes, you don't give up. Maggie said the sweetest part of the whole thing transpired a few months later. His mom passed away that year. When he got up to deliver her eulogy, he talked about how happy he was that his mom got to see him get his degree and that he knew how proud she was.

During their first few years of dating, they had started talking more about the future. Maggie asked Tim if he could hold off on all those types of conversations until she'd graduated from university. When they met, Maggie was only halfway through school and she didn't want any distractions. She needed to graduate, for herself. By that time, Tim had moved on from the video store to a full-time job with good pay. He started climbing up through the ranks with a few promotions under his belt in a short period of time. Maggie was proud of him and happy that he felt a greater sense of self-confidence about himself.

One thing Maggie learned about Tim early on was that when he got mad, he didn't want to be around anyone. He was not someone who could hide his anger, and she realized his behavior was a trigger for her. When Tim got mad, he reacted the way Maggie's father had during her childhood. Maggie would dissolve into tears, which made Tim even angrier. And with her being the kind of person who needed to talk through things to make them better, it only succeeded in making him more irritable and not want to be around her. It was an awful circle.

With this happening on repeat, Maggie started to look at her own reactions when they found themselves at odds with each other. She would experience a visceral gut-wrenching reflex that prompted immediate tears. Tim would get angry and retreat. Thankfully, in times when things were going well, they were able to talk about these issues and how they felt. Maggie was able to share with him why she believed she reacted the way she did and how his behavior made her feel. Tim was able to see how hard that was on her and worked on taming his reactions. He also expressed to her that when he was angry, he felt it best not to talk to anyone until he calmed down. Sometimes that would be minutes, sometimes hours. Maggie learned to set aside her knee-jerk expectation to talk things out immediately. It didn't work with him and it just fueled his anger and irritation overall. Tim learned to temper his tone, so as not to trigger tears with Maggie. It was a long process with many trials and errors. Twenty years later, Maggie thinks they've got it down to a science. If anyone in their house is in a crusty mood, they can announce it. And then family members can question if anything they have done caused the irritability. Based on the answer, they can walk away, knowing they just need time alone. Or, they can apologize immediately, then still give the person the space they need and be open to talking about it when they are ready. Since they figured out each other's triggers, Maggie has a hard time even remembering when their conversations have escalated to beyond heated in their house.

In those times, they know they must both walk away. And within an hour, someone returns to talk with an apology in hand. Tim will say he does that more than Maggie. And Maggie will give him that. Apologizing isn't something that comes easily for her, but year over year, she has been taught how important it is in a relationship. Maggie is thankful to Tim for teaching her how important it is to be able to admit you're wrong, especially to your kids. It's all part of what she believes makes their family click so well.

Back to their dating years, once Maggie had graduated from university, they started talking about moving in together. It was a big decision for them both; two fiercely independent people. They decided fall would be the perfect time, September 1st to be exact. And so, they began looking for a place that was close enough for Maggie to get to her job in the city and for Tim to continue his commute. They found a cute apartment in the suburbs, close enough for Maggie to walk to the train, but, for Tim, still an hour and a half drive each way to his night shift job. She says he must have loved her a lot.

Maggie was living her life in the order that had been drilled into her to be the right one. Maggie hadn't jumped into cohabitation with Tim after only a few months. They were two years and eight months of dating before they moved in together. And during that time, they worked extremely hard on their relationship. Maggie told him there was no way she could see herself in a marriage and with a life like her parents, Jim and Tina. Maggie knew that life was too short to be miserable every day like them.

Earlier that year, Maggie and Tim had parted ways for a while. Maggie had found herself thinking about the future, knowing she'd have to make some choices as her university career came to an end. That's when she'd flipped into decision-making mode. What came out of that was an honest and difficult conversation.

Maggie sat down with Tim one day and took his hands in hers. She told him she had done some soul searching, she loved him, that he was a great guy. She added that he would make a great husband someday, but she didn't think that he would make a great husband for her. She worried that once the honeymoon phase was over, that things would be good for a few years but eventually she'd have regrets and resentment. She told him she knew exactly what she needed; someone with ambition from a career perspective, someone who wanted to set goals, who wanted to get married and have kids. When Maggie met Tim, he said he was never getting married or having kids. And there were little things too that Maggie knew were huge parts of her life that they didn't share. His response was eye-opening for her. He said, "The person you're describing, that's the person I want to be. I just don't know how to get there. Can you help me?"

Maggie knew that was a vulnerable thing for him to admit but also wondered if he was just saying what he thought Maggie wanted to hear. He assured her that he wanted to make changes. Maggie told him that she was still trying to find her own way in life and wasn't sure she had the energy to help him too. He asked again and

Maggie told him she'd give him 30 days to see if he really meant it.

Those 30 days changed their relationship forever, for the better. Maggie watched him grow and open up and think more about his future. She learned that her love for Tim soared when they were making plans and setting goals together and working on making them happen. Not to mention when he'd hit a home run in baseball, and she could proudly blush and declare that he was hers.

So, they found themselves setting goals and achieving them. The day they moved in together was the day they both fully committed to each other. Any contact with old flames was extinguished, leaving room to grow in a healthy and trusting relationship with each other. With that commitment came future plans, which included the purchase of a house. Exactly one year after they had first moved into their apartment, they crossed the threshold of their first home together.

It was a time of growth in their relationship, a time when they learned that the key to their happiness together could be found through honest communication with each other. They tackled topics that weren't easy to talk about, from childhood influences to bedroom preferences. They both acknowledged that if you can't talk about those types of things and they continue to bother you, that's when resentment kicks in and the issues become much bigger. Maggie believes that those tough years of learning to talk through everything together helped build the solid foundation that they continue to stand on today. Finding that one person you could trust with your innermost and vulnerable thoughts was paramount. The respect they had for each other was unwavering. Maggie is so grateful that he was willing to take that time with her, to be honest, to be open, and to try.

Their relationship progressed as you would have anticipated. The night before their wedding, the rehearsal party was taking place in the Presidential Suite. As guests began to arrive, they got wind that was the place to be. At one point, there were over seventy people in their room. What a great way to start their lives together, surrounded by the love of their friends. They kicked Tim out at midnight because it was bad luck for him to see the bride on the day of the wedding. Finally, just after 2 am, Maggie's maid-of-honor shooed out the last of the stragglers, saying they had a wedding to get ready for.

The next morning dawned sunny and warm. The forecasted temperature for the day was 75'F, unheard of at that time of year. Maggie felt so blessed to have been honored with such a beautiful day. They had Danishes and Mimosas delivered to their room for breakfast. And then all the girls went to the spa for some special treatment before the big day. They spent some time outside in the hot oasis and Maggie enjoyed a wonderful massage. Things were shaping up. Completely relaxed, they headed back to the suite where the hairdresser was set to arrive. Once dressed and all set, their photographer captured some beautiful outdoor photos of the girls before the afternoon ceremony. Things went off without a hitch and they departed for their hot honeymoon the next day.

As they settled into life as husband and wife, a sense of pride enveloped them, knowing how hard they'd worked to make their relationship so strong. Maggie was thrilled to see that all the signs and symptoms of an unhealthy marriage that she'd lived through as a child were nowhere to be found. Life was grand.

Her boundaries were strong with her parents, Jim and Tina. They participated in holidays and birthdays but didn't otherwise spend much time together. Tim and Maggie were content with the way things were. Maggie had noticed her relationship with her parents was cyclical. There would be an incident or conversation that would lead to her putting up very high walls, sometimes lasting as long as a year or two. And then slowly the walls would start coming down and Maggie would let them back into their lives, bit by bit. Invariably, something would happen again to reset the cycle and the walls would go up again. Every time Maggie let those walls down, she lost sight of how calm and peaceful and content she was when she didn't have to deal with their constant barrage of negativity.

Maggie and Tim had purchased their first home, with the caveat that they would find their forever home by the time their kids started school. On their regular drives to see Tim's parents, they would find themselves on the back roads, winding through new housing developments. If they had time, they'd stop and look.

After having been through countless resale and model homes, they found themselves on the doorstep of a model home in a beautiful town on the water, west of the city. Maggie crossed the threshold first, with Tim right behind. Up to then, many homes they'd viewed hadn't left much of an impression on Tim. Maggie remembers looking back at him in that moment and seeing the look of "this is it" in his eyes. As they walked through the house, it became more certain that all their boxes were being checked off. All of them except the money box. Maggie wondered how they'd afford to live there. What a fun decision that had been to work through with her.

They put a down payment on a lot around the corner from the model home and sat with their finances, wondering how they would make it happen. They were both working full time and knew they had to make more money somehow. They started checking the wanted ads and had immediate success. They found jobs together, working for a transportation company three nights a week, four hours each night. After taxes, that was an extra thousand dollars a month coming in. That was a lot in those days and went a long way in saving towards their new home. Their families weren't so convinced that it was a good idea and they listened to their objections incessantly. But, right on schedule, they received the keys to their dream home that they would soon fill with incredible memories, laughter, and love.

As Maggie and I were reminiscing together over coffee that day, their house had increased in value by one million dollars. "Take that naysayers!" she laughed. The house had represented growth for her in another significant way. The two of them moved in and became a family of four in short order. I could see, by the sparkle in her eye, that she was thrilled with the results of the decisions we'd tackled together over the years.

CHAPTER 17

Nicole (Part 2): Confabulation

The next time Nicole was back, she showed me the note she'd made in her phone identifying the spot in her story where she'd left off last. She'd finished up by telling me some stories of the help her sister had expected with her kids while they were all at Camp for the family reunion. She continued.

On the Wednesday, Nicole had needed to go into town to buy groceries for their Mexican Fiesta night. It had been decided that the two oldest grandkids would go with her and the three youngest would stay with Rob. Everyone seemed happy with the arrangements. When Uncle Tom asked if she would pick up a few things for him in town, he mentioned that Sheila was going into town as well and asked if they were going together. Nicole told him it was the first she'd heard of Sheila going, and that she'd be happy to get whatever he needed.

As Nicole was brushing her teeth, Sheila came into the bathroom. Nicole asked her if she was going into town. She said she was. Nicole asked who was going. Sheila said she and Shane and the kids, unless, with a smirk on her face, she could get Mom to watch the kids for her. And that is what happened. Sheila and Shane went into town, sans kids.

That afternoon, after returning from town and having finished prep work in the kitchen, Nicole was outside of the main lodge. She saw Jade and Martin out front of the bouncy castle. Sheila had asked her to look after Martin. Nicole asked where Sheila was and when she'd be back. Jade said she didn't know, that Sheila had just told her to keep an eye on Martin and not to leave. She asked Jade, "If you could be doing something else right now, what would it be?" Jade said the other kids had gone out on the paddleboards and the kayaks and she would love to join them. Nicole told her to go. So, Nicole watched Martin until Sheila came back about fifteen minutes later. Sheila looked around and saw that it was only Martin and Nicole and that it was clear that Nicole was watching him. Sheila didn't ask where Jade was or what Nicole was doing, she just picked Martin up and off she went.

They held the Mexican Fiesta that night, after Gladys, Hank and Victor left. They kicked everyone out of the Main Lodge and set designated tables for everyone with tortillas and salsa, forks and knives and napkins. Until then, evening meals had been cafeteria-style, free-for-all. The girls dressed in black and white as waitresses for the night, each responsible for serving a table. The boys were in charge of beverages. Nicole's oldest, Nate, was on the blender, preparing frozen margaritas for those interested. And if not, they also had Coronas with lime. For those not drinking alcohol, they had grabbed a few cases of Jarritos which were a big hit. They made cheesy chicken quesadillas with sour cream and salsa. They prepped all the trimmings for a Taco Bar, complete with hard and soft tacos, guacamole and the works. The piece de resistance, according to aunts Edna and Rose, were Rob's enchiladas. There was an energy and buzz about the dining room that the family hadn't experienced so far that week. I could tell Nicole was very proud of how everything had turned out.

Later that night, once the bonfire was in full swing, they brought out fixings for Banana Boats, not very Mexican, but very much a camp tradition. Personally having never experienced Banana Boats, Nicole stated they are a must-try with instructions as follows: Scoop a long oval shape out of a banana and fill it with chocolate chips and mini marshmallows. Replace the cut piece of banana peel and wrap in tinfoil. Throw it in the coals of the fire. After a few minutes, the chocolate and marshmallows melt together, the banana warms, and you have decadence. Anna's husband, Jimmy, had never experienced Banana Boats and stated that he was going to have a chat with his parents who had obviously neglected to share this rite of passage with him growing up. Driving home a few days later, Nicole had asked her nephew, Jackson, what his favorite part of the week was. She expected to hear about the campfires or the Scavenger Hunt or the bouncy castle, but no, he exclaimed it was Mexican Night.

A few times already that week, Nicole had wondered where Sandra was. Earlier that afternoon, she had been out with the kids on the water, but many times prior, Nicole had noticed her solo out on the paddleboard or kayak. It seemed strange to Nicole that Sandra was spending so much time alone when there were so many people she could be visiting with. I asked Nicole what she made of that. She told me she wasn't sure. She surmised a few things; she knew her mom enjoyed the solitude of the water, that it was good exercise, but she also felt that Sandra might have been spending some time in self-reflection. Camp has that effect on you.

On Thursday morning after breakfast and cabin cleanup, Nicole had gone to brush her teeth. She came outside to find their kids and Sheila's kids playing in front of the bouncy castle. She asked them what they were doing. They said they were looking after Sheila's kids. She asked where Sheila was. They said she was in the lodge. Nicole walked up the lodge steps to look in the window. She saw Sheila sitting at a table all alone, playing solitaire. Nicole's not sure why she snapped, but she did. She marched back down the lodge steps and picked up Mackenzie under one arm and Martin under the other. She stomped back into the lodge. George was surprised by her entrance as he straightened things at a table close by. There was only one or two people in the kitchen out of earshot and involved in their own conversation. Nicole put Sheila's kids down in front of her and said, "We are done looking after your kids this week." Sheila looked at Nicole, puzzled. Nicole told her that it seemed that every time she turned around, Sheila had dumped her kids on someone else to babysit, but most frequently Craig's and her kids. Nicole told her that their kids were there for a vacation too and it wasn't fair that they got stuck babysitting her kids. Nicole told Sheila that she and Craig had talked about it and it was something he wanted to put a stop to. Nicole had gone on to say that just because Sheila and her husband had decided that he could be non-existent for the week, it didn't give her the right to make that everyone else's responsibility. Nicole was responsible for five kids that week. She acknowledged that they were older, but not once had she asked for help from anyone. She took on that huge responsibility and she and Rob were living up to it. Sheila could at least look after her own two. Sheila countered that she had asked the girls if it was okay that they looked after her kids and they said it was. Nicole said to her, "They aren't going to say no to you. You're their aunt, first of all, and secondly, they are afraid to say no to you, we all are."

Sheila grabbed her kids and stormed out of the lodge crying. When the older kids saw her exit the building, they came in to see what was going on. It was then that George started yelling at Nicole, saying she had no right to yell at Sheila in front of people. Her husband is gone fishing, and she needs help with the kids. It was then that Nicole chose to walk out. She had too many of these conversations with George and Sandra over the years. The treated Sheila with kid gloves and would never do anything to upset her.

Nicole left the main lodge and went to find Rob. She needed to vent. She found him by the beach and after talking to him for just a few minutes she felt better. One of the cousins came down to the beach to say they saw Sheila crying and carrying her kids back to her cabin. Nicole said she knew, and it was because she had handed Sheila's kids back to her and told her they were done babysitting them this week. The cousin was thrilled as they had been trying to figure out how to tell Sheila the same thing. Nicole was not alone in her frustration with her sister's weeklong sense of entitlement.

Not long after her conversation with her cousin, Nicole saw Shane walking towards her. She was surprised to see him in the middle of the day. He demanded to know what was going on. Just as he said that, George walked up and suggested that Shane go talk to Sheila and that he'd join them in a minute. Shane was reluctant to go but George insisted. George then looked at Nicole and told her he wanted her to know that he was not taking sides. He had just talked to Sheila about having other people look after her kids. He also wanted Nicole to know that everything that he does for his kids, is because he wants to. She remembered saying, "Really Dad, so when you roll your eyes when Sheila asks you to do something, you're telling me that you don't feel obligated to help just to keep the peace?" He denied it and reiterated that he never feels pressured. He then shared that he was disappointed that Nicole had yelled at Sheila in front of everyone. Nicole wasn't sure what she was hearing. She clarified that she hadn't been yelling and nobody else had been within earshot. He told her it was awful to embarrass her in public. Nicole admonished the double standards that were present where Sheila was concerned and questioned why he felt it had been okay to berate her in front of people. The shocked look on his face told her he had no idea what she was talking about. Nicole informed him that when he'd torn a strip off her, the four oldest grandkids were standing right there. What George said next still mystifies her to this day. Thoroughly convinced of his own confabulation, he advised Nicole to consider the fact that he had taken her out onto the front step in private before he told her how upset he was. Nicole was stunned. The scenario had happened just ten minutes prior and he'd already recreated the story in his mind to fit his narrative. She'd had enough. She decided they were leaving the next day and told him so. Then, Nicole walked away.

She spent a few minutes clearing her head, then slowly made her way back to their cabin. It was at the very end of the path, far past the other cabins and over a small bridge. It was a nice little sanctuary away from everyone. Rob was already there with the five kids. Jade and Jordan told her they had just come from speaking with Nana Sandra. Word had traveled fast.

Nicole started to laugh and told me there was more to the story. The girls had been practicing sign language all week. Zoe was preparing to sign Twinkle, Twinkle Little Star for the Talent Show that night. When Zoe had walked in the lodge and saw Jade and Jordan from across the room, they signed, HELP US, when Nana wasn't looking. Their conversation with Nana Sandra was making them uncomfortable. Zoe understood their plea for help and went for backup. She returned promptly with Nate. They approached noisily and started talking to the girls, which ended the conversation with Sandra. That's when they'd all made their way back to their cabin.

She asked the girls what Nana said to them. They said that she was making them feel guilty for leaving a day early, that this was a visit with them too, not just Nicole's family. So Nicole asked the kids when they wanted to leave and all five of them said tomorrow. They said it felt awkward with Sheila and now with Nana too and they just wanted to be back in the comfort of Nicole's house. She reinforced the option to stay, but none of them wanted to.

A moment later there was a knock on the door and Nana Sandra came in. Nicole told her that the girls were just telling her about the conversation she had with them. She asked what they'd said. Nicole was honest and said that she'd made them feel guilty about leaving tomorrow. Sandra looked at her with the most shocked expression on her face. Noticing that, Nicole asked her, "How did you expect to make them feel?" She went on to tell her what upset her the most. That Sandra had the entire week to spend time with them but had chosen to spend more time with her other grandchildren, Sheila's kids, or alone, should not be put on the shoulders of these kids. It had been so easy to recognize her tactics, having grown up facing the same guilt trips. This was one of the first times as an adult, she'd called a spade a spade, right to Sandra's face.

Sandra deflected saying Sheila needed help watching her two young kids. And Nicole reminded her that they had five they were responsible for and hadn't asked for a thing. She said, "Well, Shane's off fishing and Sheila's all alone." Nicole asked her why their decision as husband and wife had to affect everyone else. And that's when Sandra broke out the, "Sheila has bipolar disorder. She doesn't know better. We need to help her any way we can because of her illness." Unfortunately, the entire ugly conversation happened in front of all five kids as well as Rob. Nicole wanted them to know she was going to bat for them and had nothing to hide.

Nicole was tired of Sheila's behavior being excused because of her illness. She has friends with bipolar disorder who are still nice people. In her opinion, Sheila's sense of entitlement was not because of her illness.

Sandra continued to make excuses for Sheila's behavior and questioned why Nicole never cut her any slack. She told Nicole she could try a little compassion with her, that she has a hard time because of her illness. Nicole said it wasn't about her illness; it was about being a decent human being, a likable one. Sandra said that it seemed she was getting along fine with everyone else at Camp. That's when Nicole said that she'd been told that if she hadn't come out and said something to Sheila, that someone else would have. Sandra looked like she'd been slapped realizing that other people had been talking about Sheila. She got up and left the cabin.

Later, Nicole learned that Sandra had gone to sit on the front steps of the lodge and cried. When relatives tried to comfort her, she bemoaned the fact that her girls could never get along. While behavior like this used to infuriate Nicole, it was only pity she felt now.

After Nana Sandra had left the cabin, the kids decided they wanted to go play in the bouncy castle and off they went. Nicole was exhausted and needed a break, so she grabbed a beer and was texting with her girlfriend. There was another knock on the door. It was Sheila. She asked if she could come in and talk. Nicole wasn't sure what to expect but agreed.

Sheila said she didn't realize she was dumping her kids on anyone. Nicole told her that in her life with her kids, which was over fourteen years at the time, she had asked their parents to look after them twice. Sheila had asked them to look after her kids twice that day already. Nicole told her she knew that Shane was gone, but that them making that decision between the two of them put the responsibility on Sheila to look after her kids and as their mom, that was what she needed to do. Sheila said that Nicole was making her feel like a bad mom. Nicole said she didn't feel that way, that she felt that Sheila was exhausted and didn't get a ton of help from her husband and she felt badly for her because of that. That was only a half-truth, but Nicole was trying to avoid a fight.

Sheila asked Nicole why she thought they didn't get along. Nicole asked Sheila if she wanted to have this honest conversation because if she did, she'd lay it all out on the table. Sheila said she was ready. Nicole told her that all their lives, meaning Craig and Nicole as the older brother and sister, Sandra and George treated them differently. She told her that they were always cautioned

195

to treat Sheila with kid gloves because of her illness and not to do anything to upset her. Sheila asked why they had never just been honest with her. Nicole told her it was easier to be in trouble with her than it was to be in trouble with Sandra and George. Sheila agreed with that comment.

Sheila didn't understand why her parents kept using her diagnosis as an excuse. She'd told them about five years prior she had been informed that she was only suffering from depression, nothing else. Nicole had no idea why they were still stuck on that if she'd told them otherwise.

It was the best conversation they'd had in years. They learned new things about each other and in those moments, gained a better understanding and appreciation for each other. Nicole hoped it would carry through to a closer relationship over the coming years.

That night was the Talent Show. Many of the kids had prepared wonderful little acts. Even some of the adults got up and performed. There was much laughter shared and the lodge overflowed with love.

Back when they were young, their grandmother, Helen, wrote a song for the grandchildren called Twice My Children. It was about where each of the in-laws came from and by telling the story, it symbolized their family. Being the oldest grandchild, Nicole had played the piano for all of them. The family entered it into the Music Festival where they won first prize. Some of the family members thought it would be neat if they could reprise the performance with the grandchildren who were in attendance. They all laughed nervously but got up to see what they could do. Anna had the best memory of everyone, even doing the German part for Ken, George's younger brother's kids, who weren't there. As the song neared its end and relief washed over Nicole that they hadn't botched it too badly, they looked up to see Tom and Rose and Edna all in tears. They weren't sure why at first, but then realized that this performance had touched them greatly. Nicole went over and hugged them all tightly. She looked around to find George, only to realize he'd missed the whole performance because he was looking after Martin. There were so many things she wanted to say but knew it best to keep it to herself.

The seven of them planned their departure for the next day. Nicole told Rob that she wanted to do something significant to help with the cleanup before they left, as she knew she'd never hear the end of it if she didn't. She looked at the cleanup list and chose what she felt was going to be the worst job, so no one could say she got off easy. She told Rob she'd be cleaning the bathrooms. He told her he'd help, knowing how thorough they'd have to be without even having to ask. After making her decision, she'd talked to Auntie Edna about the list of chores, indicating that she would tackle the bathrooms. Her aunt immediately told her she had done too much already. But Nicole said she wanted to do at least that to make sure they were doing their share before leaving.

After breakfast, they packed up the cabin but still had to pack the trucks. The kids wanted to do a few things before leaving too, like jump in the bouncy castle one last time. Nicole decided that was a good time to start their final chore. The bathrooms were a typical campground hub. The building was a large rectangle made of concrete blocks, split in half with a women's side and a men's side. Each had six sinks and three showers. The girls had five toilet stalls, while the boys had three toilets stalls and two urinals, that she remembers. The floors were also concrete with exposed 2x4's in the ceiling, upon which they had seen many mice clambering throughout the week. Disgusting. Hair in the shower drains, mouse poop too. She shivered in recollection.

They got to work. They grabbed buckets and gloves and cleaners and scrub brushes, you name it, they had it. Nicole would have liked a face mask, but she couldn't find any handy. To get to the bathrooms from the back room of the main lodge where she'd gathered the cleaning supplies, you went out the back door and up a few muddy steps. They led to a short path to the building. Nicole had been going up and down a few times carrying all of the supplies. Her Aunt Edna was out back getting the bucket for her to mop the floors as the final step.

At one point, Nicole was coming out of the bathroom door, walking behind the wall of trees that separated the pathway and the lodge. Sandra had joined Edna by the mop pail and asked what she was doing. Nicole stopped in her tracks. Edna said she was getting the bucket for Nicole to mop the floors in the bathrooms. Sandra said, "Oh, why is Nicole mopping the floors?" Edna said, "Well, they are leaving today and that's the chore they are doing to help with the final cleanup." The words Sandra spoke next are ones that Nicole told me she has played over and over since they were asked. Sandra asked Edna, "Is that enough? Do you think they had done enough this week in comparison to everyone else?" Thank goodness Edna said, "It's more than enough considering the year and a half they spent planning the week already." After hearing Sandra walk away, Nicole rounded the trees and descended the steps. She looked her aunt in the eye and without saying a word, her aunt knew that she'd overheard the conversation. Nicole could almost feel her aunt's arms wrap around her in a warm hug, acknowledging how awful that must have been to hear.

Nicole told me cleaning those bathrooms was a bitch. She had envisioned it taking about an hour to get through them but combined, they spent five hours. Nicole added how grateful she felt that Rob accepts her the way she is. He agreed she could inspect his side before declaring they'd done a good job. She saw what he had done in his showers and how good they looked and even went back into the women's side and did the same there, as an added touch.

Once she was satisfied, Nicole went into the lodge to get her Aunt Edna. It just so happened that her Uncle Tom was there, too. She asked them both to come and inspect. They laughed at her and told her to stop being silly. She told them it was important for her to get the sign off from both of them before they left because she didn't want anyone to be able to say they'd missed anything or done something wrong. Or not done enough. So, in their graciousness, they appeased her and did the inspections and said she had nothing to worry about.

Nicole laughed as she recalled talking to Auntie Rose on the phone the next day after they'd already arrived home. She exclaimed how incredible the bathrooms looked adding, "I didn't know that waxing the floors was on the list." Nicole cried out, "Oh no, did I miss that? I'm so sorry." Rose said, "No, it wasn't on the list, but it sure looked like you waxed those floors. I think we could have eaten off them." Nicole breathed a huge sigh of relief and laughed heartily with her.

As promised, the prizes for the five-day challenge were ordered shortly after Nicole returned home. She had brightly colored beach towels embroidered with Arctic Wake-Up Dip delivered to each of the recipient's homes. The excitement she heard in the voices of those calling to say thank you was infectious and worth every penny.

She told me that's what had brought her to me. Even with all the great memories, she still had a sinking feeling in the pit of her stomach. As much as she tried to force the bad parts out of her mind, there was an overriding feeling that to do so would be a disservice to herself. She felt a decision looming but wasn't sure of her options.

She described the ongoing pattern she'd seen with her parents, one where stories were continually twisted to fit their purpose. Their inability to take responsibility for their actions or their words was more taxing than Nicole could articulate. Something needed to change.

To me, the answer seemed obvious, but it is never my role to impart an opinion. As we worked back through the negative scenarios she'd described, the cumulation of listing them out loud in sequence opened the floodgates. She looked at me, sheepishly, and asked if I felt she was foolish for not seeing what was right in front of her. I explained that in every situation, it is simply my job to help people come to their own conclusions.

She left my office that day, confident in the decision she'd made to set clear boundaries as it related to her parents. Gone were the days of playing doormat to their projections of insecurity and unhappiness. She had her own life to live. And she was going to make it a damn happy one.

CHAPTER 18

Meghan: Eight Remarkable Hours

Meghan, like many adults I know, had never enjoyed a great relationship with her parents. I learned more about their history during the many conversations we had that *year*. She shared with me that when the time came for her to leave home, she did so on terms that left a lot to be desired. Her exit was unplanned and rushed, so she took only what would fit in a single carload.

Illustrative of their difficult relationship was a phone call she received from her mother, shortly after she had moved out. The call began with Meghan's mother telling her that she needed to get over to the house – and make it quick - if there was anything there she still wanted. It turned out that Meghan's stepfather had decided to do a little spring cleaning, which entailed placing all of Meghan's personal belongings in trash bags and hauling them to the curb.

Despite the often-challenging situations involving her parents, Meghan tried to preserve a connection with them. Her confidence waned noticeably when I asked her what motivated this. In the silence that ensued, I watched many expressions flash across her face. When she finally spoke, it was barely above a whisper. She told me that she hoped the day would finally come when she would be good enough for them. Experience had taught Meghan that when it came to her mother and stepfather, her efforts were seldom rewarded or welcomed - even when she checked every good-daughter box she could think of.

To illustrate her point, Meghan talked about her efforts to recognize each holiday. To commemorate them accordingly, she'd send cards in the mail, ensuring they were posted in plenty of time. On one occasion, Meghan's stepfather received his card several days early, a fact that Meghan's mother was unaware of. When Father's Day arrived, Meghan's mother called her, eagerly reducing her to an ungrateful little bitch, and shaming her for forgetting to send him a card. Meghan, exasperated but not surprised, told her mother to talk to her husband.

This tendency to conceal any positive actions on Meghan's part was a game her parents played for as long as she could remember. She didn't understand what motivated the tiresome trend, speculating that her parents, collectively, must not want to be given any reason to think very highly of her. They would only cave in and tell the truth about her efforts when forced to do so. The Father's Day card debacle was just one example of this dynamic - another situation where Meghan ended up paying the price. It took her mother a full month to call her again. When she did, her mother said that Meghan's stepfather had finally confessed to getting his card well before Father's Day. What she didn't say, of course, was that she was sorry. Meghan shrugged as she recounted the story, acknowledging it was par for the course.

Shortly after moving out of her mother's house, Meghan called her biological father. She hadn't lived with him for over 15 years, and their once-regular visits had become less frequent in her teenage years. "Life happened, as it tends to do," Meghan explained when she talked about the relationship. Her father had become absorbed in other things – first, in his own relationships; later, in his own family, and in raising the two daughters he shared with his second wife. For much of her teens, Meghan saw him three or four times a year at most but had always had the sense that her dad was there for her, and that he would always be if she needed him.

Upon first being thrust out on her own, Meghan called him and tried to explain what it had been like at her mother's house before she moved out. She finally admitted the extent to which their relationship had spiraled, providing graphic detail. Explaining the motivation behind her call, Meghan confessed that she was feeling unanchored, and hoped that sharing her experiences with her dad would help her find some of the balance she had been missing. While she wasn't sure how he'd react, her father's response disappointed her, to put it mildly.

"I can't fault him for taking another man's daughter and raising her as well as he raised you," was what he said.

Whether or not Meghan had expectations for the conversation, she cannot say. What she did concede is that, in hindsight, his response fell short of any expectation she might have had or could imagine having – not just for him, but for all fathers, of all girls, everywhere. In a rare moment of pure vulnerability, she admitted that, while she doubts that anyone could forget those words, Meghan has to fight every day not to remember them. Meghan had lived her entire life with the knowledge that her mother and stepfather weren't there for her, and wouldn't ever be. While painful, this knowledge had always been buffered by the comforting idea of her father, and Meghan's belief that she could always count on him. She had been wrong - again.

At the time of the phone call, things in Meghan's life were going well. She'd been on her own for a few months by then. She was happy at work, spending a lot of time with her boyfriend, and loved her new apartment – even her landlords were awesome! They filled a void she hadn't known existed. All in all, Meghan was settling into a routine in her new life and was thriving. She was considering university in the fall and had gotten into every school that she'd applied to. As the saying goes, it seemed that the world was her oyster. Meghan said she was a bit surprised by the plethora of options available to her, but she had little trouble deciding where to enroll. While she probably wouldn't have admitted it at the time, she freely confesses now that she selected the same school that her boyfriend would be attending – because it was the school her boyfriend would be attending. While Meghan acknowledges that it definitely wasn't the best reason for selecting a university, she explains that her boyfriend was one of the only constants in her life at the time, and she wasn't prepared to give that up.

Although Meghan's boyfriend practically lived at her apartment during the year leading up to university, he felt it would be best if they lived separately at school. They each rented a place they shared with two roommates, located a few blocks from one other. The seven months of living on her own and providing for herself helped Meghan settle into university life without much adjustment, but the financial side of things did prove tricky nonetheless. Because she was focused on her studies, Meghan wasn't working. This meant that money was tight - money was really tight. And financial troubles started to take their toll.

Meghan made it through her first semester, although her marks weren't great and she hated her roommates. Because she had the only double bed in the house, it was often used by her roommates to convene for their "nightly activities" when Meghan wasn't home. She knew this because they were not shy about leaving a trail of evidence, half-empty water glasses and used tissues strewn about her room. As I listened to Meghan tell this part of her story, it was clear to me that the weight of all that she'd been through was starting to catch up with her. We all have our limits, after all. Everything that she had been feeling came to a head about a month after Christmas, when Meghan's boyfriend broke up with her after three years together. Without this one human being who had been her anchor, Meghan's world seemed to come crashing down. With no one to turn to, she found herself spiraling into a melancholy that she couldn't shake.

Upon her now ex-boyfriend's insistent recommendation, Meghan turned to the school psychologist. She immediately suggested that Meghan consider a change to her living arrangements, citing residence as an option. In the psychologist's eyes, the purpose of this change was twofold: first, it would bring Meghan closer to the school, which would help her focus more on her studies. The second benefit, of course, was that it would help Meghan escape from an already-bad roommate situation. With the psychologist's help, Meghan applied to live in residence, which ultimately proved to be a turning point for her. Until then, Meghan had relied heavily on her boyfriend and his roommates to occupy her social circle. Because of this, she hadn't gotten around to making many friends at university, but residence quickly changed that. Additionally, because Meghan was on campus, she no longer struggled to make it to class on time.

Meghan visited the psychologist for one hour a week over the course of eight weeks. That's it. Eight hours in total. One day's worth of work – and the best single day of work she could have ever put in. Those eight hours not only fundamentally changed who Meghan was as a person, but they paved the way for the return of her confidence. Meghan finished the year with plenty of reason to celebrate. She passed all of her courses, but more importantly, she embraced a more positive approach to life in general, which she saw carry into the following year of classes. Little could she ever know back then how pivotal a time this would prove to be in her entire life.

Despite their earlier difficulties, Meghan decided to move back to the town where her dad lived, for the summer. He secured her a position with the company he worked for and she moved in with her grandmother. Her grandfather had passed away just before Christmas the previous year, which brought some challenges to the arrangement, but Meghan got through them. The biggest test was her grandmother's drinking and her tendency to hide it from others. This became tiresome for Meghan and she found herself spending as much time away from her grandmother's house as she could.

Meghan returned for her second year of university that fall, but things were vastly different from her first year. Meghan had rekindled her relationship with her ex-boyfriend, but after deciding to pursue a different course of study, he had transferred to a university much farther away. While Meghan wanted to make it work, this distance made it hard. Meghan was living in residence again, and her social life was never better, to the point that it started interfering with her school work. To further complicate matters on the academic front, she'd started to have doubts about her course of study. By the end of the school year, Meghan had admitted that pursuing a degree in psychology might not be the right academic path for her. She was debating saying good-bye to that program as she went back to work for the same company again the following summer.

Before she left school for perhaps the final time, there was one last thing that Meghan needed to take care of. Despite her feelings for him, and despite their shared history, she acknowledged it was time to end things with her boyfriend. As he dropped her off at the airport, Meghan chose to simply rip the Band-Aid off, for both their sakes. In the midst of their embrace, she said, "Good-bye. For the last time." Her boyfriend's confusion was evidenced by the puzzled look on his face, and in his response as he asked her "What are you talking about, Meghan?"

She told him that she'd been giving it a lot of thought, and that she knew in her heart it was time to end it; that breaking up was the best thing for both of them. They were seventeen when they met and having spent so much time together, she worried that they had never had the opportunity to find themselves. She loved him but she had started to wonder if she would become resentful of him as years passed. She suggested they go out and spend some time in self-contemplation, including sewing their wild oats, before settling down. She told him if they ended up together again after that, then great. And if not, they'd know parting ways at that time was the right decision.

Meghan boarded her flight with a heavy heart and tears in her eyes. Goodbyes are always hard, but that one was excruciating. By ending the relationship with her boyfriend, Meghan was saying goodbye to someone who helped shape the person she'd become. She was saying goodbye to someone who had shown her unconditional love for the first time in her life, and who helped her believe that she deserved it. Her boyfriend, and their relationship, prepared her for future relationships. For this, and for all that they shared together, Meghan was - and still is - thankful.

As her plane landed, Meghan knew she needed to do some soul searching in the next few months. She worked at the same summer job again, but as fall approached, she started to wonder what she was going to do next. Seeking new direction and a fresh start, Meghan updated her resume and began looking for a more permanent job in the area. She'd decided to take a year off, both to save for another year of school, but more importantly, to decide what course of study to follow. Her job search was only in its second week when she was hired as a Pharmacy Technician at the local drugstore. With that, one of Meghan's primary questions – what she was going to do for money – was answered.

At this point in Meghan's life, she rarely spoke to her mother. During one of their infrequent conversations, Meghan told her mom that she'd decided to take the year off to figure things out. Her mother, certain that Meghan was wasting yet another year of her life, didn't hold back. It took just four words for her mother to share her opinions – about both her daughter's plan and of her daughter's drive and work ethic in general. "You'll never graduate university."

While this was shocking to hear, and even though the words were clearly intended to wound, Meghan decided to view them as fuel, to use them to a higher purpose. Deep down, she suspected that her mother hoped she wouldn't ever graduate university, as it was something she herself hadn't been able to achieve. But Meghan knew she could go somewhere better with her life. For the next five years, one while working and the next four at school, she played her mother's words on repeat in her head.

"You'll never graduate! You'll never graduate! You'll never graduate!" "You'll never graduate university!"

That soundbite became Meghan's biggest driver on days when the going got tough. In the years that followed, no matter where she was or what she was doing, she played it. When things were hard, she played it to help her stay on track and focused. When she felt like she couldn't take 'it' anymore – whatever 'it' was – she played it to keep her motivated. "You'll never graduate university." That's all it took. Meghan would run her mother's words through her head, and just like that, all her resistance to "getting the job done" was gone, swept away as if it had never existed at all. If there was one thing Meghan was sure of in her life, it was this: she was never going to give her mother the satisfaction of being right about that.

Meghan stayed in town through the winter, living in her grandmother's basement, which doubled as a small apartment. She saved the money for a DVD player, an expensive investment back then, and recorded television shows to watch at night. Thanks to this arrangement, Meghan lived like a hermit that winter, working during the day and retreating to the basement at night. While there were upsides and downsides to the reclusive lifestyle, it gave her plenty of time to think, deeply, and to reflect on some of her life's biggest question marks: Who did she want to be? What did she want to do with her life? What kinds of people made her happy? Meghan decided to use these winter months to expand her mind, and her world, as well. She visited the library in town and obtained a list of classic books. Within a few months, Meghan had made her way through the Top 25, still a proud accomplishment.

While she spent a lot of the winter isolated, when Meghan did venture out of the basement, she was sure to consume copious amounts of alcohol, as well as poutine – which she loved. Between these two vices, it didn't take long for her indulgences to show up on the scale, and Meghan's weight ballooned to more than 200 pounds. While the extra weight was new to Meghan, she doesn't remember even noticing at the time. Looking back on it, she says the weight really didn't seem like a big deal to her because there was something else consuming most of her attention that winter – finding herself; getting to know the real Meghan.

She became steadfast in her ideas of good and bad, digging deep into her soul to get at the heart of who she was, and, more importantly, what she truly believed. This was the winter that taught Meghan what authenticity felt like, and how to recognize when she was hiding from inconvenient truths, or wasn't otherwise being honest with herself. She figured out what excited her, what motivated her, what pissed her off, and what resentment felt like. Perhaps most importantly, Meghan learned that happiness was a choice people made, not always the easiest, but a choice to take the path of least resentment.

Over that winter, Meghan took a long, searching look at what her parents brought to the table, focusing on their positives and compartmentalizing the good and the bad. Her goal was to recognize the good in them, to emulate that, and to simply let the rest go. Meghan didn't want to deny where she'd come from, and she didn't want to forget her roots. She simply wanted to live a life free of the negativity her parents were dependent on, and that her childhood had been steeped in. She made a promise to herself, to not let her parents' mistakes become her mistakes; to not carry any baggage through life that wasn't truly her own. Meghan vowed not to live in the long shadow of their misery.

Contrary to her mother's belief, Meghan did get her thinking straightened out. She decided to go back to university to study Business, a practical career path with good job potential. This also gave Meghan an opportunity for daily human interaction, something she already knew she needed from a career. Early that summer, she was accepted to university in a city she'd never before lived, hours from home. Meghan proudly had a new attitude and outlook on her life, and that acceptance letter meant that now she'd get to live it.

So it was, that Meghan boarded a bus and began the long journey to her new life at university. This time, she had the clarity and sense of purpose she needed, and no one could stop her from succeeding. For four years, Meghan focused intently on school, and on succeeding, while she completed her honors baccalaureate degree. Because she'd changed programs, she had to forfeit most of the credits she'd earned at her last school, but that wasn't a concern. What did matter was that her life was her own, and it was up to her to make it a success. For the next twenty years, that was exactly what she did. The teachings from those eight hours she'd previously spent with the psychologist were paying off in dividends.

During our very first meeting, Meghan acknowledged that things had recently taken a downturn. They must have, since here she was, deciding, after all this time, whether she should seek therapy again.

Having spent the majority of her adult life as the focused, driven woman Meghan was after returning to university, she had recently been reduced to a mere shell of herself. She understood what had created this rift between the woman she had worked so hard to become vs. the woman she was unfortunately regressing into: her family. A variety of interactions had transpired with them, each one resulting in their unfavorable judgment of her actions. How did she know it was unfavorable? They didn't hold back. Phone calls and text messages that would curl your toes, each blow hitting harder than the previous. As an adult, Meghan had to be careful about the boundaries she kept with her parents and siblings, but because of the recent events, Meghan seemed to be carrying more and more of their negativity with her. At one point, while she was still able to recharge between hits, she felt she was going to be okay. But the last few had been so vicious, her recovery time so elongated, that she didn't know if she'd make it. She had begun to question who she was, where her life was going and no longer exemplified the confident woman she had decided to be that winter in her grandmother's basement. She had taken such pride in becoming who she needed to be over the previous twenty years. Why was she stumbling so unsteadily now?

As we worked through her options, I could see clarity begin to dawn in her eyes. She was a proud and strong woman, rarely seeking or asking for help. I could see her acknowledge how beneficial just our short conversation had been. Not only had it provided her with an immense sense of relief to unload that burden of how she was feeling, it encouraged her to see her situation through another person's lens. The factors she listed of importance to her became the reasons she decided to try therapy, once again. It had worked for her the first time, so many years ago, why not try anew.

A few weeks later, she followed up with me via email. With a referral from a trusted friend, she'd nervously scheduled an appointment to see a psychologist. Since then, they'd already met three times and she informed me of her progress.

In just one session, Meghan said she was feeling so much more like herself again. The cathartic process of retelling her stories and subsequently losing the weight of each one she was carrying, was impactful. She went home after that first session with such a sense of relief, she'd immediately scheduled a second appointment.

Through her conversations with her therapist, Meghan was able to acknowledge the reality of the situation with her family. Her next step was to redraw the boundaries that her family had been crossing more and more frequently as time passed. This decision, to start choosing herself again and stop sacrificing her happiness to her family, was all it took to get Meghan back on her feet.

CHAPTER 19

Elizabeth (Part 2): F&#ktard

We left off our last session with Elizabeth with her family on their way to her dad's for Christmas. Elizabeth's relationship with her dad's wife, Gail, had been rocky and awkward to date, even after 20 years.

And so, they arrived on the 23rd. The next afternoon, on Christmas Eve, they met up with Elizabeth's aunt and uncle and cousins and went skating at the outdoor rink. They kissed them goodbye as they left and said they'd see them in a few days as Gail had planned a big sleigh ride for everyone on the Monday.

Christmas morning came and went uneventfully. Santa had spoiled everyone and the kids were playing with their new toys. Elizabeth helped Gail in the kitchen in the afternoon, getting ready for turkey dinner. Elizabeth recalls drinking a vodka and cranberry at the time and Gail asking her to pour her one as well. Elizabeth wasn't heavy-handed with either of their drinks, just about an ounce of alcohol in each large glass. In the kitchen, they started talking about Elizabeth's work when Gail insisted she should consider real estate. Elizabeth told her she knew it would be something that she would be good at, but in previously exploring it, someone reminded her that she'd be giving up her evenings and weekends. With two kids at home, it was still important for Elizabeth to spend as much time with them as she could, especially with their sports and activities. She also mentioned that the city where Elizabeth lived was inundated with real estate agents and it would be a hard place to get started quickly. Gail said that she should pick a town outside of the city she lived in and sell real estate there. Elizabeth told her that would kind of defeat the purpose of working from home if she was always in another town. She wouldn't know anyone there and she didn't want to sell real estate anyway. Gail ended the conversation by strongly stating that she thought Elizabeth should sell real estate. Elizabeth didn't really know what to make of the whole situation.

Before supper was served, Elizabeth refilled their drinks one more time, so they were both on their second. Going on their third hour and second drink seemed fairly slow-paced. They enjoyed dinner at the dining table, Frank and Gail at either end, girls at one end, boys at the other.

After dinner, the kids were getting a little restless and asked to be excused. While Rick and Frank were in conversation at the other end of the table, Gail looked directly at Elizabeth and said, "I need you to know that I've only slept with two people in my life; my first husband and your dad, and I'm okay with that." You can imagine the look on Elizabeth's face. Shock. To say it was an awkward moment was, as Elizabeth described, an understatement. Not knowing how to respond, Elizabeth took great solace in being interrupted by her daughter right at that exact moment. She then got up and cleared the table. The dishes were done without further conversation and it was time for Tiffany to have a shower. Elizabeth went downstairs to get her a towel and her pajamas out of the suitcase. Gail followed her downstairs and asked if she was okay with the conversation they had earlier. Elizabeth told her it was a bit unsettling and unsure what the point was.

Elizabeth couldn't remember where the conversation went next, but at one point she had said, "Gail, I'm not sure if you remember, but my mom remarried and they had two kids in their new marriage. Frank married you with your two kids and you became your nice little family. I didn't feel like I belonged anywhere." Gail told her she should have gone to live with Sally, the woman from Frank's previous relationship, since Elizabeth loved her so much. Elizabeth was fuming. Gail was bringing up Sally and it had been 27 years.

Gail stormed up the stairs yelling and screaming the entire way. Frank leaned over the railing to ask what was going on. With eyebrows raised, Elizabeth informed him, "She just brought up Sally." He said, "Are you kidding me?" By then, Gail was in their bedroom. He went in after her and the yelling and screaming continued. They were still yelling when the kids finished their showers. The four of them huddled in the upstairs bedroom together, trying to distract the kids from the noise, who had no idea what was going on. This was foreign to them. It went on so long that the kids started to cry. Elizabeth and Rick took them downstairs to the room they were staying in, in an attempt to get them away from the noise. Elizabeth reminded me this was still Christmas night.

By then, Frank and Gail had come out of the bedroom, so they had to walk by them to go downstairs. In passing, Rick asked if they could perhaps keep it down because they were upsetting the kids. But the fighting continued, so they put the kids to bed downstairs and turned on the tv. They had already decided they were leaving in the morning. This was not a Christmas that anyone deserved, especially the kids.

A while later, Frank came downstairs and Elizabeth said she thought it would be a good idea if they talked about what had happened. Frank agreed and asked what she had to say. Elizabeth suggested that Gail should be part of the conversation since she had started it all. Elizabeth shook her head, and told me that she could tell by the look on Frank's face that it hadn't even crossed his mind. He went upstairs to get her.

Gail came down the stairs, "guns-a-blazing" as Elizabeth described, yelling her way down each step. Elizabeth sat in shocked silence. Frank suggested that everyone take turns. "Gail, obviously you have a lot to say, so why don't you go first?"

The filth that came out of her mouth is something Elizabeth will never forget. She called Elizabeth the most horrible, despicable person she had ever met in her entire life. Gail then launched into a litany of every awful thing she could think of. Elizabeth continued to sit in stunned silence. Gail's rant reached far back through the years. It was clear she had been bottling up her feelings for a long time. One theme centered around a recent type of exercise Elizabeth had taken up. At the time, pole dancing was a popular fitness trend and she had joined with a group of her girlfriends. It was excellent strength building and she had made some great new friends in the classes. But Gail, and Frank, viewed it as something unspeakable for her to do, especially with children of her own.

Gail continued on with her stories, glancing at Rick as she brought up Elizabeth's previous boyfriends. She'd ask him if he knew about certain situations, bringing up things that had happened twenty years prior. And in Elizabeth's defense, Rick told her he'd already heard all of the stories. Elizabeth thinks Gail's goal was to somehow catch him off guard hoping to drive a wedge in their airtight marriage. Elizabeth sat there acknowledging how much Gail was again projecting her own insecurities onto others.

Gail brought up many anecdotes that Elizabeth had never shared with her directly but had obviously been reported back to her by her daughters. These were stories that Elizabeth had told to them in private, many years earlier, in an attempt to build a closer relationship with them. Elizabeth realized they'd shared every detail as gossip, with their mother. In contrast, Elizabeth had never shared the stories her stepsisters had privately told her over the years, with anyone. Recalling Gail's dinner table statement about her sleeping partners, Elizabeth wondered if they had been planning some sort of sex intervention for her.

Elizabeth just sat and listened. At one point, she recalled Gail saying, "All families fight. They fight and then they make up and everything goes back to normal." She looked at Rick and said, "Doesn't your family fight?" Elizabeth felt so sorry for the barrage unleashed on him that she finally spoke up. "In the almost twenty years that Rick and I have been together, I've never seen them fight, so there's been no need to make up," to which Gail replied to Rick, "Well, isn't your family just fucking perfect." Rick said, "I think you've gone a little too far, Gail."

When it was Elizabeth's turn to speak, Gail had a comeback to everything she said. She accused Elizabeth of not knowing her dad very well. Elizabeth said, "Gail, I moved out when I was five. I think we've done pretty good considering." Elizabeth didn't bother to point out the reason she didn't spend a ton of time with him was

219

because of her. As tempted as she was at the time, she sensed it might have sent Gail completely over the edge. Gail accused Elizabeth of not liking her, so Elizabeth reminded her, on the night she and her father were married, she asked him if he was happy. He told her that he was and that was good enough for her. Apparently, that was not a question Gail felt appropriate, her insecurities jutting out even more prominently by that point.

They got onto the topic of how Frank and Gail put money in the bank every Christmas for the kids' education. Gail made sure Elizabeth knew that it was her physical doing, not Frank's. Elizabeth said she knew how forgetful Frank was and of course she knew it was her. Then Gail looked at Elizabeth and said, "They aren't even my grandchildren." Elizabeth felt like she'd been slapped in the face. Here was the woman who had expressly called her before Christopher was born to ask if she could be considered a grandmother. And now she was throwing it back in her face. Elizabeth told her those were far-reaching words and gave her ONE opportunity to take them back. Gail affirmed, "Well, they're not."

Elizabeth was done. She said they were leaving and then went to pack. Gail started yelling again, then ran upstairs as Frank followed. Rick and Elizabeth finished packing, but because it was so late by that time, they decided that leaving first thing in the morning would be best since the kids were already asleep.

They could hear Frank and Gail still screaming at each and then heard the front door slam with more yelling outside. Gail was going to her sister's.

After she left, Frank came back downstairs. He and Elizabeth sat facing each other on the couch, engaging in a deeper conversation than they'd experienced in a while. Elizabeth asked her dad if he felt the two of them had a good relationship. With them not having lived under the same roof for over 30 years, he said they'd done the best they could. Elizabeth took the opportunity to share her view of Gail. She told her dad she felt like the two men in Gail's life who had meant the most to her had been taken away from her, out of her control. It left her feeling insecure, and it was unknowingly ruining all subsequent relationships in her life. Gail was one of the most jealous people Elizabeth had ever met. She surmised it stemmed from what had happened to Gail in her life and that maybe some counseling would help. That's when Frank told her that Gail still accused him daily of stepping out on her; when he went for coffee, to the gym, curled, ran into someone he knew when they are out, everyone was a potential threat to her and their marriage. Elizabeth had grown to feel sorry for Gail but also frustrated that she didn't recognize her insecurities and the impact it was having on those around her. Then, Frank said something to Elizabeth that was the saddest thing she thinks she'll ever hear come out of his mouth. He said, "I'm too old to start over." Elizabeth thinks it was the worst thing you could ever hear a parent say.

The next morning, they packed the truck to leave. Gail had returned during the night, noisily waking everyone from their sleep. She would not leave her bedroom and asked the kids to come in and say goodbye to her before they left. Elizabeth was fuming. Gail now wanted to love and hug the kids when the night prior, she exclaimed they weren't her grandchildren. Elizabeth didn't feel she deserved one second of their time. They left for what

Elizabeth knew would be the last time as she vowed she would never step foot in that house again.

After arriving back home, Elizabeth thought it might be a while before they heard from Frank. She didn't expect it to be that long though, as he had called religiously every Sunday. Finally, in March, after three months of silence, Elizabeth called him. She told him that HIS grandkids hadn't heard from him in a while and were wondering why. Frank told her they were healing and would reach out to her when they were ready to talk. He asked her to never call their house again, that he would call when he was ready. Elizabeth asked what she had done to deserve his silent treatment. He said he'd call sometime and hung up.

A few more months passed before he surprised her with a call. And it wasn't a call to discuss what had happened or how to move forward, it was simply a call that left her with the same impression she'd always been left with from them. They were going to sweep it under the carpet and move forward like it had never happened.

If you knew Elizabeth at all like I do, you'd know that didn't sit well with her. Unresolved issues eat at her from the inside out and continue to do so until they are at least brought into the open and discussed. But, in this case, Frank would not engage in conversation.

So Elizabeth played it his way, hoping she would be able to put it behind her as easily as it seemed he could. Each summer up to then, they would take the kids on a vacation for a week - camping or to a summer resort. The call came asking for the kids' schedule. Elizabeth told Frank it wasn't happening that year. He asked why not. She told him that until she had proof that Gail had dealt with her issues, she would not see the kids again. He asked her what she was talking about. She reiterated the insecurity and jealousy issues, coupled with her declaration that they weren't HER grandchildren. Frank said it would be fine, they just wanted to take them camping. Elizabeth said, "Can you imagine if by chance, you go to a campground and a long-lost girlfriend of yours happens to be camping four spots down. Gail would lose her shit. If she behaved like she did at Christmas when Rick and I were there, I can't imagine what her behavior might be like if we weren't around. Absolutely not."

It was during that call when Frank told Elizabeth how Gail felt and what bothered her most. Gail said she never felt welcomed at their house. Elizabeth asked if there was a reason. Frank said it was because the spare bedroom was never ready for them when they arrived. Elizabeth shook her head in disbelief. She laughed as she told him why she no longer prepared in advance. In the past, she would carry her guests' luggage downstairs only to find her kids had built a fort in the room or decided to start a new craft project. Countless times she wound up having to rewash all the bedding to remove the sparkles and feathers and cookie crumbs. So she made it a rule to make the bed the day guests arrived, so they'd have a nice clean bedroom to sleep in, with no surprises. If Gail had asked about it the first time, instead of being insecure, she would have learned that from the start. Elizabeth could not believe that was an issue.

To this day, the kids have not spent a week with them again and they've only been to visit a few times. Gail's brother lives in the next town over, so she assumes they stay there. Frank will call and arrange to take the kids for the day. He drives to their house, stopping to drop Gail off at a coffee shop on the way. He grabs the kids, then goes back to pick her up to continue on to do whatever it is they have planned. Elizabeth thinks it's best that she doesn't come to their house. She has no desire to see her or talk to her. Gail's negative energy is so debilitating.

A few years after that fateful Christmas, Elizabeth was still struggling. The one thing that had selfishly made her feel a tiny bit better about the whole situation was the name that popped into her mind each time she thought about Gail. As juvenile as it was, Fucktard was the most perfect word she could ever use to describe the mess that Gail is. You'll have to excuse Elizabeth for her potty mouth. It's something I've become accustomed to but may be more shocking to others. I edited the others out but could find no suitable substitute for this seemingly well-deserved title.

We continued to discuss each interaction and examine Gail's presumed subconscious motives behind her behavior. Even after pondering all the factors she was taking into consideration; Elizabeth still wasn't sure which option would prove the best course of action going forward. We decided she needed to attempt one final conversation with her dad.

She waited for Frank's next call, because she still, to this day, hasn't been given permission to call there. After some catching up, she brought up what she really wanted to discuss. He informed her that Gail doesn't think she did anything wrong that night. She said she had a few drinks and doesn't remember what she said so she's not willing to talk about it. Elizabeth could not believe she couldn't see the ramifications of what she did that night? What she did had caused the rift and silence. Frank reiterated that she doesn't think she did anything wrong and he can't make her think otherwise. Elizabeth asked if he was okay with how things are between them now, hardly ever talking, not seeing the kids. He said, "Well, that's the way it's going to be because she's not going to apologize or admit to doing anything wrong and there's nothing I can do about that."

Elizabeth countered, and asked her father if their girls have kids now. He answered yes and she asked him, "Do you consider them your grandchildren?" He said, "Of course." Elizabeth said, "Even though they are your step grandchildren and there is no blood relation?" He replied, "Of course." She then questioned, "So, would you ever say to them that they are not your grandchildren? The same words that came out of Gail's mouth about my children?" There was silence. Elizabeth thought, in that moment, the enormity of those words had finally hit him. He said softly, "No, I would never say those words." Elizabeth knew she didn't have to explain how deeply those words had hurt her. Of all the awful things Gail had said about her that night, the only words that still rang strongly were the ones she had spoken about her children. Mama Bear was out in full force that night and, to this day.

Elizabeth told Frank her biggest disappointment was people acting however they please and not taking responsibility for it. That's how she still felt about Gail. From start to finish that Christmas, it was all about her. And she still didn't have the humility to admit that she did anything wrong. The kids could continue their one-day visits with her that happen every few years until they are old enough to make those decisions and ask to see her, which may never happen. Elizabeth told Frank she was not going to facilitate and repeated that she believed Gail needed professional help to assist in dealing with the grief she never processed.

Looking back on that conversation, Elizabeth acknowledged to me that she shouldn't have been so surprised by his answer. He is a people pleaser and had been all his life. He certainly wasn't willing to rock the boat, especially where his wife was concerned. Maybe she was surprised that he wouldn't even do it for the sake of his grandchildren, his own flesh and blood.

In the meantime, Elizabeth didn't want her kids exposed to Gail's toxicity and unhealthiness before they were equipped to deal with those kinds of people. Unfortunately, everyone would lose. Frank was hurting because he doesn't see the kids very often. Before that fateful Christmas, he used to come down on his own for a week or so to visit. That invitation remained open and he has taken them up on it, but with less frequency. Elizabeth assumes there is some kind of repercussion for his solo visits. But again, you can't just act out like she did and then expect things to be hunky-dory. That doesn't work in Elizabeth's house.

CHAPTER 20

Jennifer: Bob's Your Uncle

Jennifer came into my life late that year, after dealing with extended family dynamics that left her wondering if it was all worth it. She started her story where it had all begun to unravel, when her Nana, her grandmother on her mother's side, was turning ninety.

She had called her Uncle Bob, her mother's younger brother, a few months in advance to inquire about any celebrations they might be considering. When he said nothing had been planned, Jennifer offered to take charge. As the eldest grandchild this was nothing new; she had found herself organizing family events on more than one occasion.

Sometimes those events went well. Other times, they didn't. During the less successful times, Jennifer was often amazed at the bizarre behavior of her family members and the resulting drama and gossip that inevitably ensued. Jennifer had seen her fair share of it but, this was an important day in her Nan's life.

Her Uncle Bob extended his beautiful home on the river as the venue. Since they had recently moved in, it had become a central meeting place for their extended family. It was ideal as it was closest to their Nana and could comfortably host a large group. With all the children, grandchildren, and great-grandchildren, they were now up around the 50 mark in numbers.

Jennifer's early preparations began with research, as she completed requests for certificates wishing their Nana happy birthday from their Prime Minister, Governor General, Lieutenant Governor and Premier. She also started letting family members know to save the date. And, as if this weren't enough for one person, two of Jennifer's cousins were having babies that spring, both expecting girls. She was planning a surprise dual baby shower for them, also scheduled for the day after the birthday party at Uncle Bob's house.

Jennifer's younger cousin, Sheila, her Uncle Bob and Aunt Gloria's daughter, became the local point person for the event. She had recently moved back home and had all of the family email addresses from a recent party celebrating her father's 60th birthday. It was decided that Jennifer would draft the emails and Sheila would send them out. Together, Jennifer and Sheila determined menus and bar requirements, decorations and seating arrangements. Things were planned well in advance, and there was considerable excitement leading up to the weekend.

On top of the rest of the planning, one final piece still needed to fall into place for Jennifer to feel preparations were complete. She and her Nan shared a special flower. When Jennifer had graduated, from both high school and university, her Nan had presented her with gardenia corsage to wear with her graduation gowns. It was a very special gift, beautiful and oh, so fragrant. If you've never smelled a gardenia up close, you're missing out on one of life's great olfactory experiences. At Jennifer's wedding, while they had chosen traditional rose corsages and boutonnieres for the wedding party, she had commissioned a special gardenia corsage for her Nan. Jennifer will never forget that day, seeing her Nan approach wedding guests and family members to proudly and cheekily inquire, "Did you get a corsage? Oh, is it made with roses? I got a gardenia." Jennifer smiled as she told the story, obviously very fond of the memory. She was proud of that bond with her Nan and knows that gardenias will always be one of the little things they share.

Her planning hit a small snag when she discovered that gardenias aren't in season in April in the north. Jennifer couldn't even get one shipped to her from sunny California! It was suggested that she find a gardenia tree and snip off one of its biggest blossoms to make the corsage; a perfect solution. She tracked down a tree and delivered it to a florist, who created a beautiful corsage for Jennifer to present to her Nan at the party.

So many little details had gone into the planning, and with this last detail now in place, Jennifer was finally able to relax and look forward to the upcoming festivities. Sheila had been instrumental in helping her, getting all of the food coordinated at the house, and even preparing much of it herself. Jennifer was glad to have had that point of contact up north and to have worked alongside Sheila to make it a special weekend for everyone.

The day of the party arrived, bringing with it plenty of laughter and merriment. Cousins visited and played together, some not having seen each other for quite some time. Love could be felt in each room. That evening, after the candles on the cake had been blown out and the celebration was winding down, Nan said a few words of thanks to everyone for coming. Jennifer did the same, followed by another cousin, before Uncle Bob got up to speak. He thanked Sheila for all of her hard work planning and organizing the event, he thanked everyone for coming, and then ... he sat down. Jennifer was speechless, and as she caught her husband's eye, he could clearly see that something wasn't right. With the speeches over, everyone went back to what they were doing. Jennifer, still reeling, had two cousins approach her separately to ask what she'd done to piss off Uncle Bob. She was stymied.

Jennifer and her husband stayed long after everyone was gone, tearing down birthday decorations and exchanging them for baby shower decorations for the next morning's party. This had to be done without tipping the new moms off so it was a late night. The next day, the baby shower, complete with games and prizes, went off without a hitch. Everyone agreed the morning was filled with love and fun, a perfect welcome for the new babies.

As much as Jennifer had enjoyed the shower, the memory of Uncle Bob's omission the night before still preoccupied her. Hoping to get some clarity, Jennifer had snuck in a quick conversation with her mother that morning, to see if she could shed any light on the situation. She wondered aloud if Uncle Bob was upset about something. When her mom asked why, she brought up the previous evening's speech. Although her mother hadn't noticed the oversight, she told Jennifer that she wasn't surprised, as it was characteristic of her uncle to behave this way. Jennifer learned that it was common for him to show favor with his daughter at any opportunity, warranted or not. Sheila could do no wrong in his eyes. Her mother went on to say that he kept Sheila on a pedestal, and Jennifer noticed her mother roll her eyes as she spoke. Whether the gesture was conscious or not, the sentiment was obvious.

Jennifer made a decision on her drive home that day, one that took the form of a promise to herself. She was done helping plan family events. That weekend had been the last straw and she knew it was time to pass the torch. As the eldest grandchild, she'd taken on this responsibility with good intention, but it had served its purpose. There were plenty of capable hands in the form of younger cousins who could now step in and take over. Confident in the choice she made, life moved on uneventfully.

Six months went by without reason for Jennifer to reach out to her uncle; in turn, six months passed without any interaction between them. Even after all that time, Jennifer could not deny that his words (or lack thereof) still stung, but she still couldn't figure out why it bothered her so much. In an attempt to put her mind at ease, she'd had another conversation with her mother and one with her aunt, also Uncle Bob's sister. It was she who suggested that Jennifer call him, believing he was most likely unaware he'd done anything wrong.

Taking this advice, Jennifer called her uncle, anticipating they'd talk through the situation so she could put it behind her. Whatever hopes she had for the call were quickly dashed. Instead of finding common ground, Jennifer found herself in the most awkward and uncomfortable conversation she'd ever had with her Uncle Bob. They were friendly of course and shared a few pleasantries before Jennifer explained the reason for her call. She described her perception of what had transpired six months earlier and shared how she had been feeling ever since. In response, her uncle assured her that he never meant to single anyone out and that of course, he appreciated all she had done for the party. He told her he was sorry, but to Jennifer it seemed hollow. With nothing more to say, she thanked him for his time. Had the conversation gone differently, it might have made her feel better, but it didn't. She didn't feel any better. If anything, she was more confused.

She thought back on the conversation. If he hadn't meant to single anyone out, why had her uncle specifically thanked Sheila for all of her work, essentially singling HER out? Evaluating her reaction to her uncle's words, Jennifer could see that she was in a very unforgiving place. She recognized that her brain and her heart could probably benefit from a break from her family. She readily admitted this, first to herself, and then to me, later on.

Jennifer believed that her decision to distance herself was probably one of the best she'd made for her emotional health in a long time.

She didn't interact with her extended family over the next year or so. During this time, no one else stepped up to the plate to organize any family gatherings or celebrations, that she was aware of.

One afternoon, out of the blue, Jennifer was bombarded by several of her cousins asking about her plans. When was she arriving for Sheila's wedding, and where would she be staying? Jennifer was momentarily confused, but it didn't take long for understanding to dawn. The wedding they were referring to was a surprise to her because she hadn't been invited. A line had clearly been drawn in the sand, and it would be a permanent one. She was hurt, she was mad, and she was forced to acknowledge that the situation bothered her much more than she wanted it to. Once upon a time, she'd been very close to her Uncle Bob; she would even have said he was one of her favorite relatives. But now, she felt he wasn't able to see past the end of his own nose.

The more Jennifer thought about things, the more she asked herself why. Why couldn't she accept everything in her life, and just let it be? Why did she have to take things so personally? Why did she have to let every little thing that her family members did cut her to the core? Why did they even matter?

Then the questions turned outward. Why had no one called her to explain why she wasn't invited? Why had her own mother not stuck up for her? Why did everyone continue to sweep every hard conversation under the carpet, causing years of ongoing pain?

As these questions raced through her mind, Jennifer realized that she needed to talk to someone. She wasn't able to find the answers she was seeking on her own, or rely on her husband's help anymore. That's when Jennifer found me.

Our discussions took us down a winding road through her past, as she recalled memories of the good times she'd had with her family, while also rehashing some of their more unbelievable conversations.

As Jennifer revisited these stories, we talked about how her various family members factored into her life. After one such conversation, I asked her to consider this option: What it would feel like if her family members weren't there anymore?

Jennifer took a moment to consider the question before replying, and when she did, her answer was simple: relief. In this one word, Jennifer discovered the answer she'd been seeking; she finally understood how she had to move forward.

CHAPTER 21

Tracy (Part 3): When Does it End?

For our final session, Tracy promised me she'd finish with enough time to also discuss the decision she was facing. She told me she'd been giving the situation a lot of thought since our last chat and wouldn't leave without knowing her exact next steps. I referred to my notes to remind her that she'd left off just after her wedding with the story about her favorite quilt that she'd discovered in the dogs' bed.

The next big stage in Tracy and Trevor's married life was the arrival of their first child.

Early in the pregnancy, Tracy's father called to say they wanted to buy a stroller as a baby present. And, Trevor's parents wanted to buy a rocking chair for the nursery. They were both wonderful ideas and Tracy jotted them down in a journal she'd been keeping of her pregnancy.

Shortly before the baby was due, Wendy called to say they had decided to buy a stroller as a gift. Tracy had to tell her that her father was already getting that gift. Wendy was indignant, saying that's what she had wanted to get. When Tracy didn't budge, Wendy thought about it for a moment and said, "Okay, we'll buy you a rocking chair for the nursery." And Tracy had to tell her that Trevor's parents had already claimed that gift. Tracy gave her a list of other items and Wendy said she'd consider the options.

About a month before the baby was born, Tracy's friends threw a baby shower. Wendy had RSVP'd along with some aunts, her cousin, and her grandmother. But they arrived forty minutes late without a reason for their delay.

Tracy learned later that Wendy called Trevor's mom to let her know that SHE wanted to give them the rocking chair. Trevor's mom, being the quiet, non-confrontational person that she was, simply agreed. Then Wendy asked the aunts and the cousin and the grandma to go in on the cost of the rocking chair with her. Her plan was to buy the rocking chair on the way to the shower, but the store was out of stock. They had to go to another location which was also out of stock. The result was a gift certificate. And that's why they arrived late.

Trevor's parents hadn't decided what to buy them, so Tracy told them to go ahead and get the rocking chair, and she would use the gift certificate for the change table they still needed.

The baby was due on a Saturday. The following day was Mother's Day and Tracy was looking forward to celebrating it for the very first time. But the baby had a different plan.

Instead of being able to enjoy that Sunday as her first Mother's Day, she remained anxious for the baby to arrive. And, to make matters worse, Wendy called with an agenda. Tracy said she could hear in her mother's voice that she was not in a very good place. Wendy was feeling sorry for herself and said, "I don't think I've been a very good mother." Tracy told me she didn't display much compassion in her response for a few reasons. She was in her own world of impatience with her pregnancy and the truth was, she agreed that Wendy had not been a very good mother. It was not the right time for this kind of conversation, but Wendy pressed the issue. Tracy finally told her, "I'm overdue and I'm not happy. I have other things on my mind besides you needing to hear that you were a good mother. I've got to go." And she hung up. Tracy still cannot comprehend Wendy's selfishness.

As time passed, they mostly visited Chuck and Wendy solely so they could spend time with their new grandson. During this time, the walls started to come down a bit. Looking back, Tracy thinks it was grossly propelled by societal expectations that parents need to give room for the grandparents to form bonds with the grandkids. Tracy was unaware of the negative pattern she was falling back into until two summers later when Tracy was pregnant with their second child, they rented a cottage together. It was after that week she and Trevor vowed that they would never share accommodations with them again. And, to this day, they've never let each other down on that.

Having grown up with the name Tracy, which is also used for boys, Trevor and Tracy established a set of criteria for naming their children.

Their names had to explicitly indicate if they were male or female. Tracy hates getting mail addressed to Mr. They also had to be names that when you read them, it was clear how it was pronounced. And then there was the issue of family; more specifically, their family dysfunction. They decided to choose names that did not exist within a few branches of their family tree. Another criterion they still giggle about today is the children could not have the same name as anyone they'd previously dated. She remembers Trevor making a list of boy's names, only to sheepishly shake her head as she reviewed his list. He finally requested that she make a list that he could choose from.

Tracy was on the phone with Wendy that morning from the hospital, letting her know the baby had arrived, that it was a girl, and what they'd called her. Wendy breathed a huge sigh of relief exclaiming how happy she was that they had not named her what they had originally mentioned they were considering. Tracy was used to her mother's disapproval.

A night or two after they arrived home from the hospital, Wendy called again. She had been talking to her mom, Tracy's grandmother, about how she and Trevor had chosen to spell their daughter's name. They didn't like it. They had decided her name should be spelled differently and wanted Tracy to change it. Tracy said her birth certificate paperwork had already been submitted, and that it was too late. But Wendy said it's never too late. Tracy ended the conversation saying they would not be changing it. Both of their kids' names do not have the orthodox spelling, and Tracy said that makes each of them a little more unique.

Over the years, Wendy would watch Tracy interacting with her children. One day she said, "You're so affectionate with your kids." It seemed to surprise her. As a mom, Tracy knew no other way than to express her love to her kids with touch and connection. It wasn't something she's learned, but it was certainly something she felt.

It was during this time that Tracy's cousin, Trina, was expecting her first child. When Wendy and Tracy were discussing the upcoming arrival, Wendy said, "Shirley (Trina's mom) must be so happy, expecting her first grandchild" Tracy questioned, "What about Paul (her stepson)'s boys? Those are her grandsons." Wendy replied, "I mean, her first REAL grandchild." Tracy was horrified. She said, "So Paul's boys aren't real?" Wendy said, "You know what I mean. Trina is her daughter and Paul is her stepson." Tracy replied by asking, "Is that how Chuck feels about my kids, that they're not his real grandchildren?" Wendy was silent for a minute and stammered, "That's different." Tracy wouldn't back down. "How is it different? It's exactly the same. You can't say things like that without thinking about the ramifications." The conversation ended quickly.

Fast forward a few years. Tracy's relationship with Wendy and Chuck remained tenuous. Their kids were tweens and saw them a few times a year. Early one September, Tracy got a call from Wendy telling her Gloria had died. Tracy didn't really have much to tell me about Gloria, other than when her stepfather Chuck was still working for the power company, he had knocked on an older woman's door to let her know of a service interruption. How they became fast friends, Tracy didn't know. Gloria had lived in her house for a long time and had been a bit of a packrat. Over the years, Chuck cleaned it out for her. Tracy vaguely recalled stories of stacks upon stacks of newspapers lining the hallways, akin to the tv shows about hoarders. Chuck spent a lot of time with Gloria. There were times when Wendy came to visit the kids alone because Chuck was with Gloria. Tracy used to call them the two G's - the things that kept him away from his grandkids - Gloria and Golf. When Gloria got too old to continue living on her own, Chuck looked after selling her house and moving her into a seniors' home just around the corner from where they lived. The day Chuck

239

learned that Gloria had died was the same day he received confirmation that the blockage in his intestines was a four-inch tumor - secondary melanoma. He'd had a melanoma spot removed from his head about four years prior followed by a year of intense treatment. Tracy was sure that had been a hard day for him.

Closer to the end of September, Tracy got a text from Wendy informing her that Gloria's memorial service was happening that afternoon with the time and the location, a two-hour drive away. She wondered why she was getting that text. She had never met Gloria, she didn't even know her last name. She replied, Ok, hope it goes well. She immediately received a text back that said - It might be nice to send a text to Dad. All her life, she's had her mother telling her what to do and how she should behave. Tracy was done with it.

She needed to vent so she texted Trevor and told him what Wendy had said. She smiled as she told me what a peacemaker he is. He told her kindness never hurts. She texted back and said but lying does. If she reached out to Chuck, she would be pretending she cared. She didn't care. All Gloria was to her was someone who took Chuck's time away from his grandkids. She considered texting, but she didn't have it in her. She knows she has some work to do in that area. Every text she wrote in her head did not sound genuine, so for her, that was a sign that a text was not meant to be.

Chuck's surgery was scheduled for the first week of October. Tracy knew they would be headed down to the hospital the night before, so she texted Chuck that night to wish him good luck. She had also sent him a picture of some of his buddies from high school that someone had recently posted on Facebook. He replied saying thanks.

Within an hour of sending a text to Chuck, she received a text from Wendy informing her of Chuck's upcoming surgery the next day. It wasn't surprising to her. They would have been no further than ten feet away from each other the entire time. Their lack of communication skills was apparent. And, Chuck wouldn't have let Wendy know she texted because neither of them seemed willing to admit that Tracy could do something right.

She did not respond to Wendy. She had already sent good wishes meant for Chuck and he had received them.

Chuck's surgery was postponed twice over the following two days which ended up being the Friday before the long weekend. Tracy and Trevor had made plans to visit Trevor's dad. Tracy dug deep as she considered visiting Chuck in the hospital instead. But all she envisioned was feeling fake and awkward, not wanting to be there. She was beginning to see that her interactions with Wendy and Chuck were coming to an end. Her cup was empty. She made a conscious decision not to visit him and she felt at peace with it.

Wendy texted updates and Tracy responded as they came through. She learned that Wendy's sister, Laura, had come to town to spend some time with her and help with Chuck. Soon after Laura arrived, Tracy received a private Facebook message from her, which was unusual itself. She asked if Tracy planned to see Chuck on the weekend. Tracy replied, she did not. She knew there had been a conversation between Laura and Wendy discussing her absence and she was tired of the manipulation coming from all sides.

Chuck had some post-surgery complications that extended his hospital stay. Tracy received a text from Wendy that Lori had been sending mini-videos of the kids talking to Grandpa to cheer him up these past few days, telling Tracy that a text from her kids would probably do the same.

To some that may have seemed like an innocent request, but it pushed one of Tracy's biggest buttons. There was their daughter, Lori, being perfect, again. And then there was Tracy, who could never live up to their expectations. It was a lot to read into one text, but the culmination of so many years of never feeling like she was good enough for them had left its mark.

Tracy did not respond to Wendy, but she did share Chuck's contact info with her kids and told them she was sure he would love to hear from them. Her daughter chose to text him. Her son did not.

Wendy sent about six more texts over the next two days. In one, she asked Tracy to relay a message to her daughter, in another, she was talking about all the laundry she was doing in the hotel bathroom. Tracy texted back on the Thursday letting her know that she'd passed the message on along with an offer to come out to the house to do laundry if necessary. She never heard back.

A few weeks had gone by when Tracy finally received a text from Wendy. Among other things, she said she loved her as she loved all her children. She said she knew Tracy was hurting, she was sorry, and that she couldn't fix that.

Tracy may have warmed to the message if it had not been for one small detail.

When Trevor got a new phone with his job a year and a half prior, they gave their son his old phone and number. Everyone in their family had been made aware of the change. In Wendy's typical manipulative fashion, she took the text that she had sent Tracy and copied it to Trevor's old number which unfortunately landed in their son's hands.

Tracy took a few days to consider her response. She asked Wendy to please be careful of the recipients of her texts because she should not have had to explain to her son why he was getting a text like that from his grandmother. It had worried him that his mom was hurting in some way. Tracy concluded her response by saying she was working through things and asked that she please respect her need for distance.

In analyzing the situation, Tracy felt that if someone from the outside read Wendy's text, they might think it was a nice warm message. Tracy knew it was a simple action by Wendy to assuage her own guilt. Tracy also believed the fact Wendy had felt the need to copy the message to Trevor, was telling. Wendy wanted others to believe that she was being the good person and that Tracy was the bad one, not accepting her olive branch.

When Tracy talked to Trevor about what he thought about Wendy copying him on the text, he laughed and said, "Well, they know I'm the intelligent one, the compassionate one. They know I'm the most reasonable." They never discussed it again.

Chuck and Wendy reached out to their grandkids shortly before Christmas, letting them know they were going to be in the area and asking if they could take them for dinner. The kids made all the arrangements and put together their presents. Tracy did not want any contact, so she arranged not to be there when they came to pick them up and drop them off. It was better that way.

The kids said the evening went fine. Her daughter told her that they had recently had Chuck's test results come back and everything was clear, no signs of cancer. Tracy was sure that was a big relief for them. Her son's recollection of the night made her a little sad. He said it was nice, but he worried about his manners the entire time. His exact words were, "I was afraid to do something wrong, like scratch my knife on the plate. I didn't want to do anything to set them off." Tracy asked him if that was because of the stories she'd told of growing up and he assured her, no, that it was because he'd been reprimanded before because of his manners and he didn't want to experience that again. Tracy wondered if it was worth it to have her son in a situation where he is aware of every little move he makes instead of enjoying the time? Tracy remembered her days of growing up when she was worried about her every move. Now she was seeing it happen with her kids and she didn't like how that felt.

As we came to the end of all the examples she could think of to provide the full picture of what type of personalities she'd had to deal with over the years, she appeared to be sitting taller in her chair. The weight of the memories she had been carrying was more than she'd realized. I could see clarity in her eyes. She knew she had a decision to make. It should be easy to pinpoint what her options were and without me even asking, she listed them. She told me she could keep things status quo, keep riding the same hamster wheel for the rest of her life. She could also put up some temporary boundaries until she felt better about where their relationship was at. Or, the final option she listed, she could implement some strict boundaries that she would be fully in charge of.

Option one did not appeal to her at all. She was sitting in front of me because she knew something needed to change. Option two had seemed to be the one she was leaning towards and she surprised me with her determination in dismissing that option as well. She told me in retelling the stories it had become so clear. She had set boundaries and she needed to be in control of all interactions. She finally knew herself well enough to know that time would pass, and without any negative interactions, she would start to feel better about their relationship. She would question if it really was as bad as she had remembered and chide herself for being so unforgiving. She would subsequently relax the boundaries and in short order, find herself right back at square one, feeling inadequate and never enough. She'd been there before, too many times. She could clearly see the vicious cycle that she had fallen victim to for years. She whispered, "Never again."

You own everything that happened to you. Tell your stories. If people wanted you to write warmly about them, they should have behaved better.

Anne Lamott

Conclusion

Not long after completing this manuscript, I was in our storage room going through some old boxes and came across my notes from university. Leafing through them quickly, one paper caught my eye. It was the final task from my 4th year psychology class, Models of Personal Growth. The assignment was on Personal Growth Analysis, inviting students to use the works of three theorists studied that term and apply their principles to their own life. The major problem that I had identified in my paper involved my relationship with my parents and how I would like to see that change over the next five years. The paper was ten full pages and printed with a dot matrix printer, which made me giggle. It was dated December 1995.

I'd received 20/20. A+. Excellent and was very curious to see what I'd written. As I sat amongst boxes, I read paragraph after paragraph, fully engrossed in the story. And as I reached the end, I was in disbelief. Although I had written the paper more than twenty years prior, I could have just as easily written it the week before. Not a single thing in our relationship had changed.

I wonder if the silver thread I alluded to at the beginning of the book became clear to you along your reading journey. For some, it might have been obvious, especially to those who know me personally. For others, it may come as a surprise. The commonality of these stories is twofold: not only was I the decision expert leading the charge; I was also every single woman telling her story. Every event, both pleasant and ugly, happened in my life, it happened to me.

I'm not naive. I know that everyone has their own memories and perceptions of what's happened in their lives. Even so, it was always surprising to me when, recounting stories of my childhood, my mother and stepfather would look at me with incredulity, informing me that I had remembered it all wrong.

I know for my family; I will never tell the right story. Upon accepting that reality, I realized it was time to write the book that had been percolating in my head for years. Being exposed to their destructive comments and unhealthy actions continued to be the only vortex to my past. I wanted to get off the rollercoaster ride.

It's not my intention to hurt anyone, simply to share my story. And in doing so, if I change the trajectory of just one person's thought process, it has served its purpose.

And now it's your turn.

You might be thinking that making decisions is something you "should" be able to do on your own. But when fears and uncertainty kick in, you can start to waffle and delay.

And, without knowing how to make confident decisions, you can start to put your needs and desires on the back burner, again.

That's exactly why I created The Decision Smith System, a five-step process and proprietary App that guides you through the toughest life decisions with confidence.

One of the biggest benefits of using a proven process is the peace of mind you enjoy knowing that you've weighed every option against every factor. This is not something you can accomplish with a pros and cons list.

Whether you're ready for a purge of your own or you simply want to fine-tune your own decision-making skills, the resources below are available to support you, as am I:

The Decision Smith App – Available in the App Store and Google Play, free with in-app upgrades

www.yearofyouchallenge.com – A FREE, 5 day reset designed to give you a taste of what can unfold for you when you take full responsibility for living your best possible life. No charge, no spam, just love.

Book Clubs – Do you belong to a book club? If your group reads this book (or any of my books) as part of your book club, complete this form to request my presence at your discussion, free of charge. Participation will be capped each month.

Key-Note Speaker – Does your company, team or group need some help with decision making? Hire me for virtual or in-person, one-hour sessions or day-long workshops customized to your needs. Reach out to me – here.

And, at the time of publishing, here's what's coming next:

Decision Smith Coaching Certification – Learn how to walk your clients through The Decision Smith Process yourself – complement your own offerings and portfolio by helping them make great decisions. Request to be added to the notification list – here.

'The Decision To...' series of books:

The Decision to Hire – how to use The Decision Smith System for hiring and to navigate one's personal career path.

The Decision to Buy – how to use The Decision Smith System to buy or sell property.

Be the first to know by following The Decision Smith on Instagram, Facebook and Twitter.

The Decision Smith System

During the writing of the book, I waffled back and forth between telling a story and teaching you how this system was implemented in each chapter.

I landed on keeping things separate because to me, your ability to resonate with the story might have been impeded by stopping to learn in every chapter.

What it all boils down to is that for each decision, a simple 5 Step System was followed. Options and factors were considered each and every time.

Here's a rundown of the **5 simple steps**...

STEP ONE: Identify your DECISION.

STEP TWO: List your Options.

STEP THREE: Define your Factors

STEP FOUR: Rate your Factors

STEP FIVE: Score your Options

If you want to learn more about how to make the best use of this system, our **Decision Making Blueprint** is available here.

If you're ready to make that tough decision, simply plug all of your information in The Decision Smith app. The result is a mathematical score and percentage pointing you in the right direction.

The Decision Smith App is available in the App Store and Google Play, free with in-app upgrades

Acknowledgements

How many of you actually read all the acknowledgements in a book? I'm going to assume it's not a large percentage. I'm also going to assume you don't plan on reading my acknowledgements either. I'm actually fine with that.

To me, acknowledgements are really only between the author and the recipient of the acknowledgement. What do you really care who I want to thank? The only people who pay attention to the acknowledgements are the ones being acknowledged. It's a rather selfish exercise on both sides, in my opinion.

Here's what I'll tell you. I'm pretty good at letting people know in real time the impact they've had on me, whether it be a small gesture or a lifetime of friendship. So, I decided to simply write a list of names of people who had an impact on this book, in one way or another. Some of them may be my homies who have been with me through thick and thin. Others might be some of the characters alluded to in the chapters. Lots are people who have simply touched my life in some fashion.

If you see your name here and you've been a positive part of my life, I'm most likely referring to you. Cheers friends! Duplicates are purposeful.

Mike, Zack, Hayley, Margaret, Bill, Kirsten, Travis, Billy, Tanya, Drew, Leslie, Erin, Jayne, Norma, Tom, Linda, Gary, Glenn, Michael, Cameron

KP, Leslie, Kathie, Melissa, Amber, Anne, Mary, Amy, Jane, Kelly, Salony, Angela, Cathy, Sarah, Sandra, Ishrani, Edith, Cathy, Patricia, Alex, Stephanie, Gina, Ashley, Sonia, Far, Michell, Michaela, Anju, Jennifer, Sherri, Joanna, Angela,

Sherry, Margo, Vaneesa, Amy, Kelti, Taunya, Rebecca, Jill, Cary

Amin, Ola, Craig, Matt, Claude, Trevor, Dez, Steve, Jake, Simon, Bill, Carlo, Doug, Rich, Ian, Tavis

Heather, Madeline, Meredith, Lori, Louise, Millie and Lorne, Mitch and Melissa

About the Author: Dana Peever

One of my greatest passions is to help women make confident decisions that align with the life, business, relationships you really want to have.

Making decisions may seem like something you "should" be able to do on your own. But when fears and uncertainty kick in, you can start to waffle and delay.

Overwhelm causes stress. Procrastination leads to missed opportunities. And staying stuck – well that just plain sucks.

Without knowing how to make big, tough decisions, you can start to put your needs and desires on the back burner.

Thirty years ago in university, I was introduced to a hugely onerous decision matrix and it was at that time that I realized the importance of and need for having a system for decision making in my life – that didn't make my brain hurt!

This is why I created The Decision Smith 5-Step System AND Proprietary App.

One of the most valuable benefits of the process is the peace of mind, knowing that you've taken everything that matters into consideration. It's kind of like a pros/cons list – on steroids – but better! The rest is history.

I've used my system personally to make dozens of tough decisions and I look forward to helping you become a decision-making pro very soon!

~ Dana

www.ingramcontent.com/pod-product-compliance
Lightning Source LLC
LaVergne TN
LVHW051358080426
835508LV00022B/2887